BRAVING THERAPY

BRAVING THERAPY

RAPE, BURIED TRAUMA, AND THE TRIUMPHANT JOURNEY OVER PTSD

L. FEIG KNIPE

ISBN: 979-8-89316-881-5 (Paperback)
ISBN: 979-8-89316-893-8 (eBook)

To Rion Kweller, Ph.D.

In the most difficult period of my life, as hard as this journey was,

I could feel my growth.

I knew that someday I would write about it and

dedicate the book to you.

You restored me. You have my heartfelt thanks.

To John, Alex, and Jack

My reasons for being

My anchors during the storm.

I love you beyond the stars 🩶

In Memory of Bob

Love of my life and champion of living a consequential life

You told me, "Keep up the good work."

I'm trying.

CONTENTS

Content Warning

This book contains descriptions of rape, sexual assault, mental illness, and other traumatic moments. The descriptions of these upsetting experiences may challenge your own unhealed trauma. Any such effect is unintentional, and we encourage you to seek support if you feel any distress when reading this story.

A CHRISTMAS POEM
TO NO ONE

Every year, from the time I was first married, I wrote a Christmas Poem. For fifteen years, it was included in Christmas cards in place of a Christmas letter and detailed the highlights of our family's previous year.

I did not send a poem over the first few years of my therapy. I did record this in my journal in January of 2000; however:

> Stress and sadness, pity, shame
> I didn't write when Christmas came
> I didn't say what could be said
> The rumor circuit would be fed.
> What could I say about all this?
> To others it just seems a mess.
> I don't know how we got along,
> And I don't know now how we'll go on.
> Free-flowing words just come to me.
> But nothing happy, I'm not free.
> My heart won't sing in this prison state
> My mind is filled with my own self-hate.
> Not sure anymore, that's where I am.
> I try to be happy any way I can.

But the sad truth is, I'm full of pain,
I'm stuck in it now, it won't refrain.
I've lost my way, I've lost my way.
I'll leave this for another day.
I have to remember why I'm here,
My purpose used to be so clear.
My life is not my own to live
To God and family I must give.
Everything else falls far behind
I'll do this till I lose my mind.

I was unhealthy. Sometimes I was okay, but much more of the time, I felt the way I did when I wrote that poem.

This book is my journey from trauma into mental illness and my journey out again. The journey to healing is like an epic adventure. It has its hard and scary parts, and it has its wonderful discoveries and moments of excitement and happiness. I got glimpses of my goal even when the world felt like that poem. Those glimpses told me that if I kept on with it, I would get there. I hope that, if you are in a dark world now, that this book can provide a glimpse of hope for you.

INTRODUCTION

There are many people who have endured trauma and are now suffering from the haunting craziness of PTSD. Victims of rape, especially those who buried the experience so they could get on with life, often don't leave it completely behind. It's in the recesses of the mind—the psyche. It influences everything.

I am a survivor of rape who suffered from Post Traumatic Stress Disorder (PTSD). I had been quietly going through life, handling my busy days as a mother, full-time employee at a high school, and nighttime college student. I felt like things were pretty good, even with my packed schedule. Then something happened that put me in a dark place. The rape I had experienced began haunting me after many years of the memory lying dormant. I thought I had moved on long ago, but suddenly, it affected my every waking moment, making me feel crazy.

My experience is not unique.

As a graduate student who became a therapy patient and eventually a school counselor, I have *lived* counseling for nearly thirty years. I have been in therapy groups, run counseling groups, and spent years in peer supervision discussing the repercussions of PTSD and how to help those experiencing it. I have worked with (mostly young) people who struggle with this condition. I've also helped family members (both parents and partners) who want to understand what is going on with their loved one after sexual abuse. My job was not as a therapist, but as a companion to explain the process and provide support when it got too hard.

My shared experience with others who have suffered from PTSD after rape is that something happens to trigger flashbacks that, from then on, wouldn't stop popping up. I tried to control my thinking—but couldn't. The pain and the emotions were compartmentalized for so long, and I didn't understand why I couldn't put it all away like I'd always done. When PTSD surfaces, memories of the assault are no longer controlled. Emotions appear that don't feel attached to the right things—or sometimes anything. Feeling sad, angry, and resentful because of things others don't see is overwhelming. We tell ourselves to just snap out of it, we're strong, we don't see ourselves as needing to turn to others to manage our life. I certainly felt a stigma in seeking help for what was going on in my head and the idea of opening up that private wound was scary. I wanted to share it but couldn't imagine doing so.

Even after getting over an initial fear of telling my story to a counselor for help, I struggled more recently with the idea of telling my story to the world. I was told again and again, 'Tell your story,' but I didn't want to do that for two reasons. First, I didn't want a book I wrote to have stories in it that might trigger the very people I wanted to help. I didn't want to start anyone down the PTSD road by talking about my experience. Second, I'm private, and it's very vulnerable to put your most personal information out there for the world to see.

However, I've come to realize that people who bury things like I did may eventually be triggered by something, and PTSD symptoms may start. If that person, whomever they are, needs the help I offer in this book, this is my roadmap of what to do about PTSD and what to expect.

I am also writing for all the loved ones of those who have been hurt or betrayed through sexual assault. I hope my words will help explain how insidiously this trauma affects the way the survivor sees things, feels things, interacts with the world, and tries to get their needs met. I started this book as an attempt to explain this to a friend who had struggled for years in a dysfunctional relationship with a rape victim who buried the trauma. In my career as a school counselor I spent time explaining to parents, especially mothers, what was going on with their children who had been sexually assaulted. Many women told me they wanted their daughters to just put away the experience and move on. They invariably stated that's what they had done. I knew from talking to their daughters that the relationships with their mothers often did not give them the love, nurturing, and support they craved. I hope my story changes some of that.

The benefit of telling my story and illustrating what it's like to talk in therapy is that it might raise the shades for some people. Finding a good and reputable therapist with all of the credentials is only the start. Going with your gut and knowing that you can connect with this person is the true key. Therapy for PTSD after rape is a long and challenging journey that includes revisiting your assault and all sorts of other painful life experiences that you buried. I am writing about the brave decision to enter therapy, things to know about what has happened in life to get to this confused state, and how therapy and the therapeutic relationship, expectations, and the happenstance of life all work together for healing.

The other reason I wanted to write this book is because I'm a hider, but I want to be brave. Brené Brown, Ph.D., is a researcher and expert in the study of courage, vulnerability, and shame. In her Netflix special, *The Call to Courage*,[1] she talks about the life-changing remarks she read in a speech by former U.S. President Theodore Roosevelt. He said:

> It is not the critic who counts; not the man who points out how the strong man stumbles, or where the doer of deeds could have done them better. The credit belongs to the man who is actually in the arena, whose face is marred by dust and sweat and blood; who strives valiantly; who errs, who comes up short again and again, because there is no effort without error and shortcoming; but who does actually strive to do the deeds; who knows the great enthusiasms, the great devotions; who spends himself in a worthy cause; who at the best knows in the end the triumph of high achievement, and who at the worst, if he fails, at least fails while daring greatly. [2]

Dr. Brown talked about the ways in which that perspective changed her. She went on to say:

> I'm going to live in the arena. I'm going to be brave with my life. I'm going to show up. I'm going to take chances. And...If you're brave with your life and you choose to live in the arena, you're going to get your ass kicked. (Brown, 2019, 16:42-17:05)

She continued saying that every morning she tells herself:

> Today I'll choose courage over comfort. (Brown, 2019, 17:14)

Hearing this was life changing. I heard loud and clear that I am going to fail sometimes and I thought, *Good to know. Let's get on with it then.*

I am jumping into the arena of complete vulnerability. I'm scared, but I'm also kind of proud that I'm showing courage. There are two other statements that Dr. Brown made that apply to this journey I'm on of telling you my story. She said:

> Vulnerability is the courage to show up when you can't control the outcome. (Brown, 2019, 17:59)

I don't know how people are going to see me or what they will say about me and parts of my story, but I'm telling it anyway. Today I'll choose courage over comfort.

Another bit of information from Brown's research that she passed on in a story she told applied to my difficulty talking about myself while in therapy and even what I worry about now. She said:

> In feminine norms the number one shame trigger is appearance and body image. (Brown, 2019, 33:53)

That statement stands on its own. I'm in good company in my shame, creating visualizations about a body I'm not always proud to inhabit.

I am well aware that not everyone has had a helpful experience with counseling or therapy. With PTSD however, without therapy, sufferers will just have to wait out the crazy and then bury everything again as it continues to influence and control and numb one's life. It's hard to face all the blame we've heaped on ourselves and have been trying to conceal, but not doing anything just leaves a lonely existence of forgoing love so it can't hurt us. My hope is that by reading my story, some people will be encouraged to seek therapy and stick it out through the hard journey until the very end, where great rewards can be found.

What follows is my years-long story of trying to clean up the mess that rape left me with. I've talked to people my entire life who have tried to minimize the effects of sexual assault, be it mothers who buried their own experience and wanted their daughters to do the same, or men who believe that not hearing an explicit 'No' actually means 'Yes,' or worse, that 'No' doesn't really mean 'No.' I am forever grateful to my therapist, Rion, the process of therapy, and all the people who were there for me. I prayed a lot during my years battling the demons in my head. I got very specific replies. God was reminding me that I was loved.

I wrote constantly during my time in therapy. It helped me work through how I had gotten where I was and where I was going. I was eventually able to make sense of what we were talking about in therapy sessions. It helped me start to pull up things I had kept buried. My journals were private and they were where I could be honest with myself and really start to explore. After starting the journey of writing this book, I found my journals stored in the attic. They contain a record of my thoughts and feelings throughout my years in therapy. I'm happy to have them, but revisiting them feels like tears left uncried, mingled with great pride that I got through the craziness of my emotions and life at that time. Beyond finding my journals and after I had written my rough draft my therapist sent me some of his notes as well. I've added a few of them because it's part of the therapy process from a different perspective.

My story jumps between time periods, so I've always tried to be clear in my writing about when things happened. It is not told in chronological order because my memories did not come up or get discussed in chronological order, they came when they were provoked and certain experiences were discussed multiple times, always adding a new facet to the memory and my understanding.

This work of therapy is an amazing journey for those who are brave enough and hearty enough to stick with it. I became healthier, both mentally and physically, by clearing the stress of this trauma away. I became more compassionate. I have told others that this was the hardest thing I ever did—it was a journey. It was also the best thing that ever happened to me in my life. I became the person I always saw myself as being. I realized that life is hard and that's when we learn the most.

This will be hard. That's why I'm writing to you—to support you through this difficult journey. I can't promise that everything will be better, but living in full awareness, knowing yourself, feeling your emotions, and being authentic is so worth the journey.

With Best Wishes,

Linda

THEME 1

THE PAIN

CHAPTER 1

Trigger

"Is there ever a time," I asked, "when you go to therapy and you come out feeling worse instead of better?"

It was 1998 and the end of my first summer class in Counseling Theories in my journey toward becoming a school counselor. We'd been talking about therapy in class, and I wanted to hear that there were bad therapists who make their clients feel bad. My fellow graduate students were quiet. They were all younger than I was, most in their mid-twenties. I, by contrast, was in my early forties and was recognized as having much more life experience. My professor looked at me as he said carefully, "Well, in the situation where someone has a rape in their past that they didn't deal with, therapy will be worse before it gets better."

A dozen of us were sitting in a group circle and as my professor said the word 'rape' I felt like I'd just had someone throw something at my face.

The room started spinning, and I was trying to clear my head,

Don't blink, don't blink. They'll know...

I went home from class that evening shaken. And so started my journey into PTSD. From that day on, I could barely sleep or eat, and I obsessively thought about being raped until I thought I was going to go crazy. My mind started to pull up experience after experience from eighteen years prior.

Waking up with a man standing next to my bed, climbing on top of me.

> *Stop thinking about it.*
> Hand over my mouth. "Stop screaming and you won't get hurt!"
> *Stop thinking about it. Stop thinking about it!*
> In Me.
> *Stop it! You're letting yourself think about it. Put it away.*

But the memories kept coming. Day after day. Night after night.

I started writing to try to make sense of these thoughts and feelings, but it had been weeks and I'd barely slept. I couldn't eat; I couldn't talk about it.

That is how I came to be sitting in my professor's office. I needed to know what was happening to me.

My professor was a psychologist, and I finally made an appointment to see him. I really needed to understand what was going on with me, what happened when he made that statement in class. I explained a bit of my background and the strange, intrusive memories I could no longer turn off.

I told him about my past and the break-in eighteen years before, a bit about my marriage, and the flashbacks:

> "It was such a long time ago, back in 1980. I lived alone and a guy I didn't know broke into my apartment and raped me. It was terrifying. I guess it traumatized me, but I didn't know it. Then I met my husband and he didn't understand

all the turmoil I was feeling. He thought I was screwed up from that assault so I went to see a therapist."

"You said you went to therapy?" he interjected. "Did that help?"

"No! I felt terrible both times I went to see her. My older brother said that I should feel better talking to a therapist, so I just quit."

I had been bitter for nearly twenty years about that unfortunate experience, but I never talked about it because it so badly messed with my mind.

"It made me scared of therapists. I felt like if I talked about it, people would just imply it was my fault, or say I didn't want to admit how screwed up I was. That was what my husband said to me when he was mad."

My professor interrupted me. "How is your relationship with your husband? Are you able to talk to him about stuff in your life?"

"We have a loving but…volatile relationship." That was the first of many times I described my relationship with my husband in those terms.

"Can you tell me more about that?"

"My marriage? Yes. I love my husband and he loves me and most of the time we get along fine and everything is good. Sometimes, life just gets really hard and he gets super stressed, and that's when it's more volatile."

"What do you mean, volatile?"

"Well, he starts feeling criticized and angry and he'll snap at the kids or belittle me. If he lets things simmer too long, he will rant at me about stuff he says I'm doing to make his life harder. Then things calm down and after a while everything is good again."

"Thank you for clarifying that for me."

I continued explaining to my professor, "I knew I was strong and I could take care of myself, so I moved on after I was assaulted. We got married and now we have three kids. And here I am, in school to become a school counselor."

Talking about this was hard. Unless I'm trying to help someone understand something about themselves, I don't share much about myself. So as I sat there, I was caught up in the difficulty of revealing this information.

My professor started explaining what seemed to be going on and I told myself to pay attention, not to let my mind get swept away in my intense emotions and nervousness.

"When you have a traumatic event and you're not able to fight your way out or escape, or if a memory is too awful to keep mulling it over, you shove it away. It's kind of like cleaning the house right before guests arrive—you just shove everything into the nearest closet and shut the door."

He went on to say, "Likewise, you shove stuff that you don't know what to do with into a compartment in your mind. You put the rape in there, then as other unpleasant stuff happened, you shoved it in on top of what was already there. It's called compartmentalization and it becomes how you deal with upsetting emotions in your life. But the compartment gets full and eventually, it's going to burst open and memories or sensations come spilling out. You can't control that."

This totally made sense to me. I had closets in my house where I loaded junk. Eventually, the closets got full, but when my house was clean, I'd forget about all that stuff. Then, for some reason, when the door popped open, everything spilled out. I had shoved into the compartment in my mind things I didn't know what to do with. As with my real-world closet, I couldn't just put the thoughts and feelings back in my brain closet. I would have to go through that stuff, sort it, get rid of what I didn't need, and properly file the rest of it.

My professor was pretty clear that I would need an expert to help me clean out the compartment in my head now that everything had started popping out. I was suffering from PTSD. I wouldn't be able to fix it on my own.

My first step: I finally needed to find a *good* therapist.

CHAPTER 2

Then

I was a child in the sixties and everything in my world felt a bit idyllic. Well, maybe not everything.

My grandmother was my special person in a world full of kids clamoring for my mother's attention. We called her Gane, a toddler's pronunciation of Grandma that stuck through thirteen grandchildren. Gane lived right across the street and I was at her house all the time, often for overnights in a room of my own. We would make ice-cream floats when I stayed. She read Oz books to me and told me about all the wonderful places we would travel when I was old enough. At night, I would sink into the big bed with the pink satin comforter pulled up under my chin. I felt like I was sleeping in a cloud. Other nights, back home in my own bed, I would worry about how I would ever cope if anything happened to Gane.

Gane died in a fire in her house the summer I was eleven. She was overtired from family events and was smoking in bed when she fell asleep. When Mom told me through tears the following morning. I just sat in shock. I went to my room to lie down while she told my younger siblings. My little sister sobbed while Mom held her. In my mind I scolded her, '*Stop crying! Don't you know how hard this is for Mom? You're just thinking of yourself.*' She cried, but I buried the pain. For a year, every time I heard sirens I broke into a cold sweat.

But life moved on. I had loving, kind, and successful parents and a fun family life with my siblings. I've always been well-liked, the oldest daughter in a family of eight children. We lived in a big house with kids everywhere. My older brother was active with my dad and had lots of friends. I was kind of the second mother in the household, taking care of kids, doing what I could to help…the memories of a happy childhood.

I was twelve years old when I saw Mom, in the dining room, ironing a housedress that was obviously not new, but one I had not seen before. I started with my questions.

"Where did you get that dress?"
"Your aunt sent it to me." *Well, that doesn't explain much.*
"She sent you one of her dresses? Why?"
"We share dresses off and on."

I didn't respond because everything was clicking in my mind. Stuff from the past month was falling into place.

Mom, asking me to watch the kids when she went to the doctor… *Mom never goes to the doctor alone, she only takes the kids to the doctor.*

Mom, not feeling well lately. Mom never gets sick!

Mom, wearing dresses I don't recognize!? She and Aunt Lin share dresses?

Oh my God…

"Are you going to have another baby?" This was my tentative, '*Please! Say No!*' question.

She replied, "We are."

27

I didn't say anything else, but in my mind I was thinking, *Oh damn. I'm too old for another baby.*

There were already seven of us kids in the house, and I had just started junior high.

I was twelve.

I was just a kid myself, helping Mom with the younger kids. I was kind, smart, and beginning to blossom into a slightly plump beauty, the quintessential "Good Girl," a people-pleaser. I did what I was told. I liked myself a lot, except when I didn't. There was a voice in my head that chastised me if it seemed I was upsetting anyone. I buried bad or confusing feelings. But the world was at my fingertips. In my family and maybe in my mind, I was living life on a pedestal.

Life on a pedestal is really hard to maintain.

In the early seventies, as a melancholy teenager, I can remember wistfully languishing alone in the living room, thinking about my future.

> *I'm going to end up taking a gun to my head someday.* I was struggling with a labyrinth of thoughts and emotions, sad and embarrassing. *How could I possibly leave home in another year for college and an adult life? How could I leave the littlest kids in the family? Why did I exist on the outskirts of popularity? Why didn't I have a boyfriend? Why was I so tall? Why couldn't I be as thin as some of the girls? Why couldn't I talk about all the thoughts and feelings swirling in my head? I could never explain it all, even if I tried, it all felt so chaotic.*

I didn't know why I felt this way, but I was stuck.

That was over fifty years ago, when I was seventeen, a junior in high school. Periods of sadness occasionally marred my life as a young teen. My thoughts about suicide, however, were my first clear memories of really feeling depressed.

Then I went to college and had lots of friends and a few boyfriends. I got involved in a lot of activities at school. My campus was only four blocks to downtown in our tiny, very rural college town. Downtown is where the bars were. Downtown is where we went to have fun. Downtown is where I met all of my boyfriends. I've grown enough now to know that most relationships started with alcohol are doomed to failure, but at the time, I got dumped enough to think that something was wrong with me.

Of course, there would be some depression after yet another guy would stop calling. That's normal. I had an angry and somewhat abusive boyfriend in the mix, but he stuck with me, so I stuck with him.

"Don't let him treat you like that!" My much-tougher girlfriends tried to extricate me from that tumultuous relationship. I deferred to my belief that I just had to care more, show more love, and be a better pleaser. At one point I was left bruised inside and out from a particularly injurious exchange with this angry giant who towered over my nearly six-foot frame. That was enough for me, and my girls protected me after that, refusing to pass his phone calls on to me and sheltering me from his attempts to see me. I kept my distance, but I suffered from depression and even more so stomach issues, head and chest pain from the stress of that broken relationship.

But some lessons are hard learned. I started to date a guy from a dysfunctional family and a background that included minor legal troubles. It ended in a sexual encounter that was offensive to me, yet I felt partially responsible. I thought to myself, *I'm never going to think about this again. Ever.* So I did not. That was certainly the greatest shame of my life and I buried it deep. I told myself I would never talk about it.

I still can't. Maybe later.

So I was a person who kept things to myself.

In 1977, after my college graduation, my best friend and I moved to Florida. It promised to be a delightful change from the winter cold of New York. We started professional careers, I was a social worker, she a teacher. We were adults, living on our own. We made friends, dated, and had fun. We shared an apartment until she met her future husband and moved back north. Then I was on my own in a state 1,500 miles from home. I tried to find a job anywhere closer to home and return to people I loved and who loved me. Instead, just as I was looking to move back North, I got offered a really interesting position with a magazine. I would get to travel and network, so I stayed in Florida. I got my own little apartment and started life as a single professional woman. I settled in.

It was 1980, and my new job and my life became about meeting new people. It was fun. One of the people I met was a beautiful young woman, about my age, who had recently begun a job at our magazine as a graphic designer. I wanted to become friends with her. We seemed to be a lot alike. She was quiet too.

Before I really had a chance to get to know her though, buzz started that her apartment had been broken into and she was raped. An office friend told me that she didn't live far from me and I should be careful. I didn't know her well enough to talk to her about it. I could tell those first few days, however, she was in pain.

Then, within weeks, it was *my* apartment that was broken into. And *I* was the one who was raped.

*******************1998*********************

September

I was in my first session with my new therapist, Rion, telling him what I remembered. When I let myself talk about *it,* I started to talk as though it was happening:

> "I was in my apartment, startled awake."

My voice became smaller as that scene from 1980 suddenly felt real again.

> "Someone's standing next to my bed. I yell and a hand claps over my mouth. He was saying, 'Don't scream and I won't hurt you.'
> I was thinking, *God, it's her rapist. He's here for me."*

I never talked about any of this. Not like this. I never told my husband; I never told my mother or my friends. I discovered that mostly people are as careful talking to you after you've been assaulted as they are when someone you love dies. Other than the police and the lawyers, most people don't ask you questions. The police and the lawyers don't ask how you feel.

Now I was talking about it for the first time. Slowly, haltingly. Many pauses. But Rion remained quiet to let me think. To remember.

> "I think I was in shock, but I thought if I kept talking to him maybe I could make him like me a little bit, maybe he wouldn't hurt me...I didn't want to think about what was happening."

Actually, I asked if he'd done this before. He told me, "No," but I didn't believe him. He asked if I was going to call the police and I lied and said, "No"...

"He asked my name...

"I'm so embarrassed that I did this, but I told him. I was afraid to lie because maybe he already knew and I didn't want him to be mad at me.

"Then he was gone and I was sitting there in shock and he came back...

"He dropped my keys next to me on my bed. He said, 'Be careful not to leave these in your door. Somebody could come in.'

"Then he left again. I just started to sob. I left my keys in the door! It was so stupid!"

Rion had been listening, only interrupting with a gentle question here or there. I didn't know at the time, but it would take more than one session to tell this story, to remember how it felt. I couldn't think any of it through. I couldn't stay with the discomfort that my actions may have saved me if I had reacted differently, if I hadn't left the key in the door, if I'd said different words, done different actions...

Just like my professor had said, Rion assured me that my thoughts and questions had been stored away in a compartment of my brain, so I could move on with my life. Rion further explained that I'd been piling unpleasant memories and feelings that I didn't know how to deal with into that compartment for a long time now. As life progressed and things happened that made me uncomfortable, I skipped past them. This was my existence: skipping past things that make me uncomfortable, and shoving it all in my cluttered brain closet.

There's much more to trauma than a one-time event. For me, it wasn't just the rape, it was life after rape—the new me after being raped. In those early days and years, I didn't recognize its effects on my life. That's the insidious part. For me, and for a lot of us survivors, that understanding came a lot later.

CHAPTER 3

It's Not Over

1980

I was always good at keeping things to myself, keeping things hidden. It's hard being wronged, however, and rape was too big a wrong for me to let this stranger get away with. But I knew I couldn't let him see the police at my house. I had said I wouldn't call them. What if he was watching my apartment, and would come back to punish me? So I called my boss. He and his wife were in their thirties and their small company employed a limited staff of twenty-somethings whom they looked out for and were teaching the ropes of business. They were the closest thing I had to a surrogate parents nearby and they came in the middle of the night and took me to the hospital, where I was examined and a rape kit was done. After I consented, the police were notified and arrived at the hospital. That started the legal process.

My family lived in another part of the country from me, so after leaving the hospital I stayed at my bosses' home for a few days. The night I returned to my apartment I got a phone call (before phones identified who was calling). I picked it up.

"Where have you been?"

It was his voice. The rapist's voice. It was terrifying.

Oh God, I told him my name when he was on top of me. He's keeping an eye on me. Calm down. Calm down. Just keep talking.

My head was spinning. I had to quiet my mind for this simple conversation. It was my opportunity to find out about him. There was clanging coming over the phone.

"Are you a mechanic? It sounds like you're at a mechanic shop. It's kind of late for that isn't it?" I was saying whatever I could until my thinking cleared.

"No. I'm at my job. I work second shift at a factory."

There was more small talk as I tried to settle my ragged nerves.

"So you can make calls during work? That's cool," I replied. He started relaxing a bit in the conversation.

"Not while I'm working. We're on dinner break right now."

"So you're a mechanic at a factory?" I was finally calm enough to start flattering him and maybe get information. It worked.

"No. I'm just old enough to work this shift now. I work on the wrapping line."

"Umm, you know my name, but I don't know yours."

"I'm Derek."

"So what's a wrapping line, Derek?"

"It's the box factory. I wrap stacks of cardboard."

Now I knew where he was, and my thoughts were clearing. We conversed back and forth for a bit, but I realized this conversation wouldn't prove to the police that he was my attacker, so I moved to the relevant topic.

"You know, you scared me the other night when you came into my apartment while I was sleeping. You need to knock before you come into people's houses."

"Well, that's why I called. You need to get your windows fixed because I could have gotten in through your windows. They're easy, not secure."

"Oh, okay. Thank you for telling me. I'll do that."

"I have to go punch back in now or I'll be late."

Then he was off the phone, back to wrapping cardboard.

*******************************1998*********************************

This long-ago conversation I had with my attacker I was now recounting to Rion and I was pleased with the look he was giving me. Rion was as astounded as Frank, the detective on my case eighteen years prior.

"Everything that happened was so humiliating," I said. "I'm proud that I was able to keep my head and find out who this guy was. It felt like a win."

He said, "I don't know what to say. You talked to the guy who broke into your apartment and raped you? He called you up?"

"Yeah."

"What did you do after that?" Rion seemed kind of fascinated by this unusual scenario and I felt for a moment like the heroine of a really good story.

"I called the police. They were shocked that my attacker called and gave me all that information. They came and got me and we went to the factory where he was working. I knew his first name, age, the line he worked and the time he punched back in. It didn't take them long before they brought him to the door where I was waiting. He didn't come in and I didn't see him. They just had him speak and I identified his voice."

Rion was leaning forward in his chair. "Did you ever get to look at him?"

"It was pitch black when it happened. No. I didn't try to look at him, even when he was very close. I talked to him though and he talked to me. I knew his voice really well."

"Then the detective interviewed him at the station. He told me later that this guy had been watching me and he seemed kind of obsessed with me. So I guess he was a stalker. I didn't even know I was being stalked."

The sessions when I revealed my little bit of audacity were among the few times it felt good to talk about any of this.

But the facts, along with my evolving perspective, were that I got raped, but I didn't die, so that was a win. And I caught him. I'll grant you, he wasn't that bright, but I've always considered that a win too. I spent a lot of time second guessing myself when I thought about how I responded, but I finally allowed myself to talk about it. With some reflection, I saw that beating myself up over this was a waste of time and energy. That was a third win. After all, here I am telling you the story of my journey to make myself whole again.

After the rape, I couldn't remember anything that happened in the month prior. With all the other confusion of that time, also losing those memories was really troubling. I didn't understand what was happening to my mind, so along with the trauma, my questions about my memory lapses were put away. This came out in bits and pieces as I tried to talk about my experience and seemed to struggle with the simplest details. Often my mind would go blank and I couldn't talk. I voiced my frustration to Rion and he explained it to me again and again, but throughout my time working through this, some explanations stuck and some just drifted off into space, or perhaps the closet of uncomfortable feelings. What Rion was telling me, and I now understand, is that

I shoved situation-specific memories into that compartment in my brain and shut the door.

He would explain it and I'd catch a bit of what he was telling me, though it was hit and miss that first year of therapy.

"Losing memories is not uncommon when you suffer severe stress with trauma," Rion assured me again. "PTSD is a dissociative disorder. We'll talk more about it as we continue, but that compartment in your brain where you put sensations and experiences you never thought through is what we'll be working on in therapy."

CHAPTER 4

Blocked

The trial finally took place in December of 1980. It was more than five months after my assault, and I was a witness. This was not my decision. My rapist was being prosecuted by the state as a criminal. I was subpoenaed by the district attorney's office to testify. Once my assailant was caught, I had no say in his prosecution or my legal role as a witness.

***********************1998***********************

I was trying to explain all this to Rion. Describing the legal process was a bit tedious and maybe not very pertinent to my struggles, but it mattered to me. I felt victimized and I couldn't quite convey how upsetting that was.

> "I met with the Assistant District Attorney," I said. "She was interviewing me, walking me through the details of my assault, and my mind just went blank."
>
> "Can you tell me about your mind going blank?" Rion asked.

"I couldn't remember anything. It was so strange—
nothing was there. It all just got shut off. I was in her office
answering her questions and then suddenly, I couldn't tell
her anymore. It was like my mind just went blank."

Rion was sympathetic in his response, "You were dealing
with a lot."

"I guess I could only feel so much shock. I didn't make a
conscious choice to block it, it just went to a place I couldn't
access anymore. The ADA was asking questions, I was
feeling humiliated about what I had to answer, then it all
disappeared."

My body was tingling as I put this into words for Rion: that I
had been embarrassed when answering about my actions or lack
of action during the attack, that all I did was talk to the guy.

He continued gently, "You know, when you first were
confronted by your attacker it is a primal response to do whatever
is necessary to save your life and hopefully not get hurt. For you
that meant talking to your rapist."

I winced. I hated that word—rape. It would not come out of
my mouth for a long time. Instead, I mostly just said "assault." I was
reliving the legal proceedings as I talked about what happened.

I was back in 1980 again in my mind.

I was at the lineup. There was that uncomfortable tingling
in my arms and legs—I hated that shocked feeling.

"Please don't make me see him."

The detective, Frank, came in. I liked him. He was kind.
I said, "You know I've never seen him. I don't have to see
him do I?"

"No, you just have to listen to them speak. There will be
four voices saying the same thing. You have to identify your
attacker's voice."

"All right, I can do that." *Let's just get this over with.*

He opened a door and said, "Number one."

A voice spoke. "Don't scream and you won't get hurt."

"Number two."

"Don't scream and you won't get hurt."

"Number three."

"Don't scream and you won't get hurt." *That's him!* My face, my whole body tightened, but Frank's hand went up.

"Number four."

"Don't scream and you won't get hurt."

Frank closed the door. "Can you identify your attacker?"

"Yes. It was number three."

I was shaking, trying to calm down after hearing that voice again. I just needed to hold myself together until I was alone.

Don't cry. Don't. Cry. Just get out of here. "Is that it?"

"Yes we're done. I'll be in touch. You did great."

I walked out of the police station. In my head I was calculating defense strategy. I was thinking that in multiple choice tests when people don't know the answer, they more often pick number three.

They didn't have to make him number three! They should have made him number two or number one or number four. I could've picked that voice out no matter what, but like, number three is what people say when they're not sure.

I don't even remember where I read that. Probably *Psychology Today.*

I was remembering parts of the legal process such as my deposition by his defense attorney who got to question me before we even went to trial. I don't remember specifics about this but I recall I didn't think much of his lawyer. During that meeting he asked me some inappropriate questions about my personal sexual activity. The DA stepped in and he changed his line of questioning. I was shaken. Again.

I described some of this to Rion, but some things would just play in my memory outside of our therapy sessions. I might bring them up during an appointment, or sometimes not, as was the typical course of my therapy. There was so much chaos in my head, so many memories popping up then disappearing again to wake me in the wee hours of the morning that topics in therapy were often a crap-shoot. What popped up got discussed when I felt brave enough to put it out there. When I was feeling timid, I just hoped Rion would say the right thing to allow me to open up.

The legal proceedings were clear in my memory though. It was a process that went on for months. When we finally went to trial, five months after the rape, as a witness I was not in the courtroom. I don't know what went on other than when it was my turn to testify on the stand. The defense attorney, whose job it was to defend my attacker, tried to make it look like I was culpable in some way for my rape.

I'm sitting across from Rion, remembering how unpleasant it all was.

> "Your statement says that you screamed when you woke up and saw someone."
>
> "Yes." *Where is he going with this?*
>
> "Did anyone hear you?"
>
> "Uh, I don't know."
>
> "Did you scream loudly?"
>
> "I don't know. He put his hand over my mouth and told me to stop."
>
> "Please scream for the court."
>
> "Excuse me?" *What the hell!?*
>
> "Please scream like you said you screamed that night."
>
> I was desperately looking around the courtroom while he waited. I opened my mouth, but nothing came out. I was

paralyzed in front of a courtroom of spectators. I sure as hell couldn't scream for the pleasure of the court.

"I...I..." I looked at the DA to save me, he didn't do anything for what seemed like a very long moment, but finally he stood and objected. The judge sustained, telling the defense to move on.

"Nothing further," was the defense attorney's comment.

The humiliation of this witness is complete.

I guess I was lucky that this defense attorney apparently didn't read *Psychology Today.*

The trial only lasted a few days. He was convicted on my twenty-sixth birthday.

Happy birthday to me.

I was a mess.

I was reliving this in my mind as I told Rion a very condensed version:

"So you got a conviction on your birthday? My goodness. Some gift."

"Yeah. By the time the trial was over, I couldn't forget it fast enough. I just wanted to get on with life. I don't remember that time very well, though. Then I met my husband and I can remember everything after that."

Rion sat next to a clock that clearly indicated we had come to the end of this session. He leaned forward in his chair as he wrapped things up.

"We haven't talked about your husband and your marriage much. It seems that will be a good topic to discuss at another session."

"Oh, my marriage is fine." I stated flatly. "We won't need to talk about *that*."

43

CHAPTER 5

Control

I was in my next therapy session and despite my statement to the contrary, we were talking about my marriage.

> "I met my husband two months after the trial was over." I picked up on the topic from the previous session. "It seems like my memories start again after that."

All to myself I was remembering eighteen years ago in 1981, the eve of Valentine's Day.

A girlfriend dragged me to a nightclub where I did not want to be. I was in a foul mood sitting at the bar with my arms crossed and a 'Don't come near me' look. Some men approached, but I don't remember anyone even talking to me.

Until….

> *"You don't look like you're having a very good time."*
>
> *"I promised my friend I would go out with her tonight. I'm not in the mood."*
>
> *"But you came out anyway?"*

"I told her no, but she couldn't find anyone else to come out with her, so here I am."

"You're a good friend. Can I buy you a drink?"

"I guess so."

He was the friendliest-looking guy with crinkly, sparkling eyes and an awesome voice. If I had to sit there anyway...

He waited while I ordered the drink he was buying.

"Let's dance," he said.

"I'm not in the mood to fast dance. Or slow dance for that matter."

"Okay, when the right song comes up, will you dance with me?"

"Sure."

"This song?"

"No."

"This song?"

"No."

"This song?"

Shit—he wasn't going to give up. I was conflicted, thinking, 'I don't want to send him away, he's a nice guy. I really don't feel like dancing, but then, I didn't feel like coming out tonight either, and here I am.'

"Sure," I answered.

So we danced and the song finished. I turned to walk off and sit down but he took my hand and said, "I think we should keep dancing until you smile."

This handsome guy with a wonderful voice was determined to make me smile.

So I smiled. It was all put away, after all, and maybe he was right—maybe I just needed to move on, to start dancing until I smiled. So, I put a smile on my face and moved on with my life and began a relationship with this delightful guy who was attentive and sweet to me. He always brought me flowers and he brought some joy back into my world.

Rion interrupted my memories:

"So you met your husband just months after the trial?"

"Yes. I wanted to shut the door on the whole thing and start healing."

"Did that work?"

"Not entirely. I couldn't talk about it, but it was always front and center in my mind. I tried helping at a Rape Crisis Center but I couldn't get through the training. It was uncomfortable to just sit there and listen to them talking about sexual assault…about rape. Then I went to my church and talked to the associate pastor. He was so not prepared to talk about sexual assault that it was almost funny, in a mortifying kind of way."

Once again I was lost in an awkward memory for a moment.

This isn't what I was thinking when I called for an appointment. I thought I'd be talking to Father Donahue! My pastor's gentle kindness seemed to accompany his age and wisdom.

I don't even remember this assistant pastor's name. Well, I'm here, let's do this. So I said, "Father, I came to get some help, I've been having a hard time lately."

I was tiptoeing into this dialogue and Father responded, *"What is giving you trouble?"*

"I had someone break into my apartment and he…he assaulted me. It was a sexual assault. It's really bothering me."

Father What's-His-Name was not expecting this. He started talking fast.

"I'm sorry this happened to you."

I expected his sympathy although his uncomfortably awkward demeanor made me suddenly wish I could make a dash for the door to end my own discomfort. Then he stammered, *"Shall we pray?"* and continued without waiting for me to respond.

"Dear Father in Heaven, please take away the injury from this young woman…" with many more words being prayed and flying rapidly by me.

Father What's-His-Name was invoking Jesus, Mary, and Joseph over and over to help me or forgive my sins or something. Oh my God, it was *so embarrassing*.

"The only comfort I have in that memory," I told Rion, "is that I was not the only person in that room who couldn't wait for me to leave!"

Rion hadn't said much. Sometimes getting me to talk was like pulling teeth so when I started, he wasn't going to interrupt.

He finally interjected, "So you were trying to do something to help yourself process your feelings. What happened?"

I continued explaining to Rion, "It was affecting our new relationship. I had a demanding job, which added to my low tolerance for stress and my boyfriend was navigating his own difficulties. We were both struggling, so again, I shoved all those concerns away in the compartment in my mind. I decided I was lucky and I moved on. Whenever we started to fight, I would just melt down, start sobbing, and sometimes just collapse. I know I had lots of emotions and reactions spilling all over him. He told me I should go see someone to talk about the assault, because I wasn't talking to him and I clearly needed help. My doctor, or maybe the attorney's office, referred me to a psychologist. When I went to that appointment, his wife told me that she was a clinical social worker and that she would be speaking to me instead. She decided that I should talk to a woman because of, you know, the *nature* of my trauma, my being sexually assaulted."

"Because you were raped?" Rion interjects. *I hate that word!*

"Umm...yes."

Rion and I didn't dive too deeply into my early experience with therapy. Talking through completely ineffective counseling didn't seem to be a good use of our time together. The memory made my blood boil, however, so of course my mind had me relive that following summer of 1981 and my exchange with the woman I *didn't* make an appointment to see.

She started our first session saying, "Why don't you tell me about yourself."

"Well, I'm twenty-six and I live here alone. I came down to Florida after college and now I work for a magazine."

"Oh, did you come here for a job?"

"No. I came here with a girlfriend and then found a job after."

"Where are you from? Where is your family?"

I was getting annoyed. This woman knew why I came here. I told her on the phone I wanted counseling because I got sexually assaulted. I actually thought she was a man on the phone, she was older with a deep, smoker's voice.

I answered her question, "I'm from up north. My family is all there. I have a question. Are you Dr. Edmond?"

"No," she replied. "Dr. Edmond is my husband. I'm a clinical social worker."

"I thought I was seeing Dr. Edmond. I was referred to him."

"Well, when we got your referral, I thought you should be seen by a woman, so I took your case."

This was not sitting well with me, but I let it go.

She continued her questions, "Why are you living so far away from your family? Why did you leave them all to come here to Florida?"

"I moved here with my best friend after college. Her parents are here."

I was feeling my back against the wall. Why did I have to explain my decisions about my life choices to her? What did this have to do with my assault?

She then asked, "Are you in a relationship?"

"Yes."

"For how long?"

"A couple of months."

"How long have you been in a previous relationship?"

"I guess six months."

"And you are twenty-six? Never married?"

Shit. I knew when I was being judged and this woman was judging me. There was definitely an implication there was something dysfunctional about my family or me.

Both times I saw her, she directed the dialogue and we never even talked about the sexual assault. She judged me, and never made me feel comfortable.

Rion listened to me as I described my struggles with my boyfriend and with the previous therapist. He wanted to clarify something for me about the counseling process and just my relationships in general.

"It isn't healthy in a relationship if one party is controlling. It is especially important after you were raped when you were unable to control anything that was happening. In our work together, you are in control. I am not going to direct what you talk about or try to lead the discussion. You are in control of yourself and whatever you are ready to talk about."

That understanding was helpful to me, both in trusting Rion and in unpacking my marriage. In my relationship with my husband, right from the start, we had both unwittingly needed to be in control. He blamed me and called me critical when I didn't agree with him. Being a strong personality and oftentimes confrontational, he would tell me what he believed I should think or feel. I was a strong personality, but not confrontational and would shut down against his attempts to control. He thought my meltdowns were manipulation and that my refusal to work with the counselor was because I didn't want to hear how messed up I obviously was. We argued loudly and frequently.

When I explained my relationship to Rion, I told him that there were many tears, but mingled among them were many moments of joy. We talked about our plans and our future. We sympathized with each other's challenges and life traumas, and we loved each other, even through the pain and dysfunction.

So just eighteen months after we met, we got married.

The new me after rape was who entered marriage. There was healing that needed to be done, but in those early days and years, I didn't even recognize the effects of the assault on my life. That's the insidious part of rape. It gets mixed into everything and you don't even know it.

I just thought, *Well this is life.* So when Rion and I started to talk about how being a victim of a sexual assault had played out in my life, I was confronted with those thoughts for the first time.

> I was being reflective as I said to him, "We spend a lot of time and energy trying to figure out how to get through life the best way we can. I don't usually consult with anyone about it."

I was learning on this journey of therapy that after being in a situation that I couldn't control, it affects how we relate to others. I worked hard to control anything and everything that had to do with me. There was a painstaking realization that those around me were affected by my need to control.

Rion responded, "There is a lot you just don't want to talk about."

"Yeah," I replied, "and we all have an idea of what we should do for ourselves. I don't really want anyone else's perspective. If I feel out of control, I wait it out until I can move on. I think how I was raised and what I learned from earlier experiences kind of informs that thinking. I know I am strong and I feel pretty tough. I felt lucky that I survived and I just moved on."

"You've accomplished a lot in your life. It's a credit to you that you are ready to start discussing your thoughts and feelings now. When you do that you get to add new perspectives that help you develop new insights and understanding."

CHAPTER 6

Life & Marriage

M ost nights were the same, we would make love before sleep... then my husband would quietly drift off beside me. But I couldn't sleep...

I wasn't overreacting. The physical and emotional exhaustion of tending to kids, family and work and then my husband's needs felt overwhelming. It was too much to ask of me. But this was normal, being overwhelmed. All the other moms I knew also seemed to be overwhelmed and overworked.

It was different for us, though. Those looks that said, 'I want you,' felt like lust instead of love. Is that what love is—how marriage goes—the joy of making love reduced to obligatory satisfaction of your partner's needs, regardless of your own?

I knew my husband loved me, desired me, but I felt so exposed by those looks that I got defensive and tried to deflect his overtures. My response was the opposite of what he was hoping. He would get angry and tell me I had a duty as his wife to take care of his needs. It played on my guilt. Sometimes I thought he was making veiled threats that he might have to look elsewhere for his physical satisfaction. This control caused more of my reluctance, but I got beaten down and did what he wanted. Even so, I couldn't conceal my reticence, and this caused him to question my love and commitment to him.

With every perceived slight, his anger swelled and his perception of my love deteriorated. Anything at all could begin the anger that festered in his mind. If I didn't wish him luck as he headed out to a sales appointment, he thought I didn't care how he did and it would be tucked away and brought up later. I might ask if he planned to spend the evening with us or if he'd be out on appointments, and he felt I was criticizing how he spent his time and he would berate my lack of support. If I shared my daydreams for improvements we might eventually make to our home, he would immediately take them on thinking I was trying to manipulate him into doing a project. Eventually he would be overwhelmed.

His financial and business responsibilities along with those of our home and family wore on him as the strife between us grew, but still, most nights he would reach for me to alleviate the stress of his day by making love, even if I was exhausted and sleeping. When he thought that I didn't care he would vent his rage in rants at me to try to control my behavior. He berated me until he wore out his anger and every time this happened he felt better, but I would be beaten down. He'd be remorseful, but it would be weeks before I could recover. I started living life as though I were walking on eggshells. I was afraid to say anything, to ask anything or talk about my dreams for our home. As the years and my mental health deteriorated, his anger and his rants increased.

Finally, to sleep, to dream…

Darkness is everywhere. I'm alone…
'What is that? Oh God, where can I go? Hush… Hide!'
I can't see. Everything is a shadow.

Shadow people, ghosts...
'Get out of this place! Run!'
I'm shivering. Is this my house? I'm running through hallways so dark I can't tell. It feels like my house. Chasing me, closing in. I'm cold.
'Oh. help me, God!'
I sucked in my breath as I jolted awake.
All was quiet, dark, and familiar. My room.
That dream again. That nightmare of being chased in the dark. Over and over I would run through dark halls, almost escaping. Those dreams went on and on for nearly twenty years. People were chasing me... and ghosts.
Calm. Down.

Silently I would creep out of our room and check on the boys. They were always fine, sleeping. One of them would slip under our covers before the night was out. In the bathroom after I splashed water on my face, I'd return to bed, always with the prayer,

Please, God, protect me. Let me sleep.

On the surface was a happy family, loving each other. Underneath, cracks were widening and with each shift, more cracks formed. Isolated in my failures, I couldn't share my humiliation.

Throughout the 80s we had our children. Shortly after my youngest son was born in 1989, I became a non-profit director part-time. Even though it didn't pay much, after several years we were able to build a house in the country that we loved. As our boys grew from babies into children I would watch them playing quietly, longing for the intense love I had for them when they were little. I missed it, but told myself this was normal. This is what happens when our children get older. I didn't realize the problem:

I was numb. Strong emotions were too dangerous. If you let yourself love too deeply you could get hurt and I was feeling more and more like I needed to protect myself, so I compartmentalized my love away. Strong emotions had to go.

Money was tight so in 1994, soon after we moved into our country home, I got a grant-funded, full-time job doing school-to-work programs in our high school's counseling office. As the grant was due to run out within six years, I returned to college for a masters degree in school counseling so I could be hired by a school district.

And here we've come full circle. It was the summer of 1998 and my first class of the degree program, where my professor made a statement about rape therapy that initiated my full-blown PTSD.

Once the PTSD began, I would lie awake in bed. I had lost control of my thoughts and emotions. Everything in my world had changed. It was like I wasn't living my life, I was just reacting to stuff that was not part of my current world, stuff from twenty years ago that was spilling out of the closet in my head. It was nuts.

I laid there ruminating about my dilemma.

> *Why can't I eat now? The breakfast shake at least has some nutrition. I don't know if I can keep solid food down—I can't even put anything solid in my mouth. This is the strangest thing that's ever happened to me. I love to eat. I love food and I have a cast-iron stomach. But right now the most I can put in my mouth is a little piece of peanut butter sandwich. At least maybe I'll lose the weight I'd like to drop if I can't eat anymore.*

And I couldn't go to sleep.

Then I'd start thinking about that stranger crawling on me.

Stop it!

I can control this, don't think about it.
Just pray.

I dozed, but at 4 a.m. I was again wide awake

Stop thinking about this!

Constantly tired and thinking obsessively about being overpowered and scared, the sensations of turmoil and shock derailed my functioning. I was bewildered that I couldn't stop thinking about all of it. I saw myself as strong and smart. I couldn't believe that I didn't have control of my own mind. I was feeling isolated and sad. My emotions were inappropriate for the events they were attached to and I had physical sensations that didn't seem to relate to anything. My usual escape was sleeping and I slept a lot. When the discomfort got too unbearable, I talked to close friends or my sisters. My favorite distraction was dates with my husband. We would go out for dinner and a movie once a month. We both looked forward to time together to talk and step away from responsibilities.

Everything would be fun until we were sitting in the big dark theater with a huge screen in front of us and the loud noise of the movie all around. I would start getting chills up my back and feel tingling throughout my body. My eyes would start darting around on heightened alert. I felt in my body the commotion or dilemma that was playing out onscreen.

My first year in therapy we went to see the movie, *There's Something About Mary* with Cameron Diaz and Ben Stiller. While I enjoyed the movie, the creepy sensations began for me when all of Mary's suitors were, unbeknownst to her, very obviously stalking her. I enjoyed the movie though, even through my discomfort.

Afterward, at dinner, my husband said I was like Mary, nice but oblivious. My husband was always rather jealous and thought I encouraged inappropriate attention. All the unpleasant emotions I had during the movie flooded me again (along with being flattered that my husband had just compared me to Cameron Diaz). Over my years of struggling with PTSD I realized that, among other things, movies triggered a danger response from me. I didn't stop going to the theater, but I became more discerning about movies I should avoid.

There were many circumstances that had made me consider therapy, but the severely uncomfortable sensations had forced me to action. After my unfortunate first experience nearly twenty years before, I knew I had to be comfortable and connected with a therapist who had professional expertise in the field of PTSD and sexual assault therapy.

But how did I suddenly get to a point where I didn't have control of my mind? What actually happens to individuals who are affected by PTSD after trauma? Would understanding help me get back to normal more quickly? Was there something more I could do? There was so much I didn't know about my mind and how it works. I had a lot of work to do.

With access to academic papers and college libraries, I started reading everything I could to explain what was going on in my head.

CHAPTER 7

Memory and Trauma

All my life, I've often been called a scatterbrain. At least that's what my parents and college friends and the people who knew me best said. I always found that label annoying. My memories, thoughts and feelings were organized in my mind just fine.

Or were they?

I've been mostly lucky in my life, a fun childhood with lots of wholesome experiences. There were a few traumatic times, of course, but for the most part I could put those experiences into perspective. As a well-loved and educated woman, I had the confidence after college to move far from my home and family. I had a job and a good network of people. I was lucky.

Then in 1980, the rape.

Eighteen years later, after my PTSD reawakened, I would often get sucked into different aspects of that night and the days, weeks, and months that followed. I would be washing dishes, or driving, or trying to focus at work, but suddenly, I would be consumed by a memory. Nothing came in order—memories popped up when something activated them. I didn't tell the story in order in my mind or in therapy. Remembering once didn't mean it wouldn't come up again and again with new revelations of something else that had been hidden or seemed insignificant or of a feeling that I finally recognized.

I was trying to understand how memory is stored after trauma and I started thinking about everything I was going through after the rape.

This particular memory started with the phone call I made to my boss, the night of the rape, well past midnight. I kept the lights low. I was scared, afraid I was being watched, but I was afraid to be alone right then too. Revealing the particulars of this assault to my boss was intimidating, but I had immediately made a choice not to hide the information.

"I just had someone break into my apartment."

My boss had been sleeping, but was instantly awake and questioning me. "Are you okay? Are you hurt?"

"He raped me."

"We'll be right there. Are you okay to be alone while we get there? Do you want me to call the police?"

"No! I don't want the police here. I told him I wouldn't call them. I'm okay. I'll wait for you."

Chris and James were the natural choice to call in a crisis. Chris was my direct boss, who I worked with daily. She and her husband owned a graphics company and I was hired as an account executive for literature they published. Her husband James was the publisher and my boss Chris managed the company. It was a family operation that had been growing even in the short time I had been employed there, but it was still an intimate group of people who all felt like a work-family.

I eyed my liquor cart as I hung up the phone. Someone had bought a bottle of Courvoisier Cognac to a party I'd hosted recently. It sat unopened on the cart. I broke the seal, picked up a brandy snifter (purchased from a thrift shop) and poured a shot into it. Then I waited.

Both Chris and James arrived and were in my living room. They had discussed what to do on the drive here.

> "We should call the hospital," Chris explained, "and find out what steps we need to take."

Chris called the hospital Emergency Room. She was told I should be examined to be sure I was okay. As we drove to the hospital I pretended this was just a regular medical visit. I was keeping my head and was glad my car was still at my apartment. *He* might be watching and I wanted it to appear as though I didn't go anywhere or tell anyone. I was examined in the ER and they did a rape kit. The medical staff was kind, but I was holding things in, keeping it together. A nurse collected a sample from under each fingernail. I asked her why she needed it. She said it was for any blood that might be from my attacker.

I said, "I wish I'd known what you needed. I would have scratched him." (I'm quite sure I would not have). I was making jokes because emotionally I was shutting down, deflecting from the unpleasant business at hand.

After evidence was collected and I was medically cleared I was taken to a small office in the hospital where two detectives waited to interview me.

> "Hello. I'm Detective DiNapoli. You can call me Frank. This is my partner Detective Marsh. Can you answer some questions for us?"

The lead detective, Frank, was a nice guy, seasoned in his job. His female partner, Holly, was young, very sharp, and about my age. I heard she left for the FBI Academy soon after all this. Both

Frank and Holly were kind and caring as they gathered my name, age, and address.

"Can you tell us what happened?"
"A guy came into my apartment and attacked me."
"He attacked you?"
"He, um...raped me."
"Did he hurt you?"
Hesitation... "No. I'm okay."
"So was there penetration?"

There were more questions from the detectives, but the two words that immediately shut me down were *rape* and *penetration*. I continued to answer questions but I have no memory of what they were.

Finally the interview was over and we went back to my apartment. It was already morning but I was very nervous about police cars being there. I had specifically promised I would not call the police.

What if he sees police cars? He'll know I lied.

I was scared right then. I stayed out of the way as they went through my apartment. They took my bedding.

"Is this the nightgown you were wearing?" Holly asked.
"Yes."
"Did you wear underwear? Is there some here?" asked Frank.

It was humiliating that everyone there knew what happened, such intimate knowledge about me and then they were asking about my personal habits; I slept without underwear.

"No. I didn't wear underwear."

They were gathering up everything my attacker touched and putting it in a bag. My mother gave me those floral bedsheets and my favorite nightgown for Christmas. I asked if I would get them back. I don't remember if I got an answer.

I didn't want to be where I was. I just wanted to escape. And like every other time in my life when I couldn't escape, when I was numb and in shock, I didn't think it through. I shoved it away. I spent several days away from my apartment, staying at my bosses' house. The night I returned home was the night my attacker called and was apprehended.

Finally, on night four, I was in my apartment alone, shaken and scared. My attacker was behind bars, having been apprehended the night before, but I still felt afraid. I put a large pair of sewing shears on my nightstand, it felt like a weapon in disguise. I might be able to go to bed feeling somewhat protected. I was feeling isolated however and I didn't know whether I should call my parents or wait until I went home on vacation to tell them. I needed to talk to someone so I called my older brother to ask what he thought I should do.

"Hi… How are you?" I started.

"I'm good. You don't sound great. Is everything okay?" I guess he could hear it in my voice.

"Not really. I had someone break in to my apartment a few nights ago."

"Were you there? Are you hurt?" He was calm and concerned. I felt safer.

"I'm not hurt. Well, yeah, actually. I got raped. I called because I don't know if I should wait until next week when I go home to tell Mom and Dad. What should I do?" I didn't cry because I'm tough.

He thought for a moment. "I'm coming to you."

It was late when we talked. My brother flew overnight to Florida from Detroit to be with me and arrived first thing the morning after I talked to him. I never realized how quickly someone could rush to my side from so far away. He stayed for a few days and we called my parents—he said they wouldn't want to wait to find out, but that knowing he was there with me would make them feel better about it. He put a secure deadbolt on my door. We joked around; irreverent humor about criminals and inappropriate ways to deal with awful situations. Mostly, I was just glad I wasn't alone, physically or in my head. Someone I cared about knew. I felt protected and safe.

Then my big brother went back north and I was on my own again. I just moved on with my life and didn't think about it much.

Well, that's not true.

You know how sometimes you can't stop thinking about something that you just want to go away? That's more accurate. I wanted it to go away. I wanted to not think about it. But I couldn't think about anything else.

I needed to talk to my mother.

I traveled home and followed my mother around for the entire week I was there, all the while telling myself,

Just say you need to talk.

I made small talk about what she was doing.

Say you are having a hard time. Just open your mouth and say something!

Nothing came out of my mouth. I was longing to talk to her, my mind was constantly trying to find ways to start, but I couldn't say anything about it to her at all. I couldn't tell her how scared I was. I couldn't talk about what it feels like to think you are lying under your murderer. I couldn't say how humiliating it was to have to talk about the details of this sex act with strangers in big, bright, stark rooms. Those conversations are meant for little safe spaces, with dim lights, pillows to hold and covers to crawl under. Those conversations are meant for special people who know how to listen, who know how to make it easy for you to talk, who make you feel safe. Throughout my life my mom was that person for me. She couldn't bridge this gap, though. Neither could I. This was too personal, too embarrassing, I couldn't stop thinking about it and wishing I could talk—the one thing I wouldn't do.

When I returned to my apartment in Florida, I started dealing with the prosecutor's office—the first time my mind went blank. When the Assistant District Attorney peppered me with questions I could answer, then I couldn't. We had to end the interview. Everything had become so disorganized in my brain that although I couldn't stop thinking about it, I couldn't put anything into words. It was all blocked for me. I didn't have access to the words or memories when I was supposed to talk about it.

I couldn't comprehend that I had been in the company of someone who wanted to do me harm. I had always seen the people in my own little world through rose-colored glasses. I couldn't wrap my head around having been the victim of that kind of crime: rape. I was too humiliated to talk to anyone, I couldn't even talk to myself. Talking is what puts things in perspective, talking is what leads to healing, but I would just keep feeling and remembering the sensations of what I saw, what I heard and felt, without being able to reason it out like in a normal situation. I was unable to make sense of it, to form it into words. Psychologically I was deeply scarred, but I did not have physical injuries, so I just put it away. I was not going to dwell on it. Talking was impossible, so I didn't talk about it—and I tried not to think about it, either. Eventually, it did just become something in my distant past that I seldom thought about.

It was almost twenty years later, a lifetime in young-person terms. I had my children, my husband, and my career. And it was back. The overstuffed closet of awful experiences was haunting me.

I had a strong need to understand what was going on in my brain. In one of my first therapy sessions, I asked Rion, "Why did this happen to me, if not everyone responds to trauma this way?"

I was attempting to intellectually understand this situation I was in. I usually deferred to cognitive questions when it would have been more helpful to let myself feel, and try to understand that. At this point in my journey, Rion was trying to get me back on track with my therapy, but he always let me lead.

> "Understanding why won't make you better. Working through it will."
>
> "I still need to understand what happens in my head. I've been reading about how we remember, how our brains store memories," I protested.
>
> "Okay. Let's talk about what you read," Rion acquiesced.

I liked this about him—I was in charge here.

I explained that I'd been trying to understand memory, albeit on a very basic level.

> "I read an explanation that said memory is biology combined with biography. So the biology would be the sensations from our five senses, what we see, hear, smell, taste, or feel. The biography is my story about what I experienced, my thoughts put into words. The sensations get united with the words, the story around what happened. That all gets stored as a memory in another part of the brain."
>
> "That's an interesting explanation. What else?"

Rion would always encourage me to do the talking. This kind of talk—about knowledge and learning—was easy for me.

> "Well, when you feel scared and get a surge of adrenaline it will increase your strength and speed so you can fight or flee," I responded. "Those reactions help protect you. Like your heart rate speeds up so more blood flow can oxygenate muscles for strength. Pupils get dilated to improve sight and hearing is more acute. Stuff like that."
>
> Rion confirmed, "You do become hyper-vigilant. You can't control those reactions."

Knowledge is power and I was feeling a bit less crazy. The validation that those reactions were out of my control was helpful. Working with someone who could help me reprogram my brain was better than trying unsuccessfully to do it on my own.

We were getting close to the end of our session and this discussion, at least for the time being. Rion was wrapping up.

> "You're not abnormal for feeling these things. You are not abnormal for developing PTSD. It's a response to trauma that happens to some people. We might be able to revisit the science of it another time if it seems like it will help."
>
> "It's helping me to understand why this happened," I persisted.
>
> "I know that, but remember, the *Why* isn't going to help you get better. The more time we spend discussing why, the less time you're spending feeling the feelings you are trying to avoid." Rion reiterated. "I'm sorry, but we are out of time for today."

I always watched the clock. It was frustrating to have to end a session when I was finally talking, but I could see for myself that we were out of time. Often I was disappointed in myself that I took so long to start talking, and annoyed with Rion for being so meticulous about time.

He stood and I followed him to the door.

CHAPTER 8

PTSD

****************1980***************

After my assault—the rape—my office colleague told me about the assault she suffered in our shared neighborhood. I thought we had the same attacker, but as we talked, she described her attacker as physically very different from mine.

"Have you gone to the police?" I asked.
"I tried to resist every way I could. I fought him and he got on my back and he raped me anally."

I was shocked by her blunt admission. She continued talking and I just listened, with unspoken feelings of familiarity. I was surprised she was telling me this.

"I've been to the doctor and I've got damage—tearing, and stuff. But no, I haven't gone to the police,'" she said in reply.
"Will you do that?" Her reporting wouldn't help my case, but I pressed a bit, because I think I wanted confirmation that reporting this crime was the proper course of action.

"No. I just need to move on. I'm having a hard time just going to the bathroom. I don't want to talk about it to people."

She was flat in her description but firm at the same time. She was struggling enough dealing with the trauma and its aftermath; pursuing it legally would have been too much to bear. It wasn't long before she moved away. I was sad for her. She fought, and *that* happened. I couldn't imagine.

I thought about my experience. I hadn't fought, and wasn't able to flee. I didn't really do anything except try to placate him, because I thought doing so would give me a better chance of not getting hurt. There was not a lot of similarity between our assaults, other than the fact that the reactions we used in the moment, though different, did not save us from being raped.

Feeling terrible for my colleague after hearing her story, I thought that I should feel lucky because I didn't get physically hurt like she did. Mine was still a terrifying event, of course, but at the time I didn't believe that my feelings were justified. Compared to a lot of rape victims I felt fortunate. I shouldn't take up space with my emotions and should just toughen up.

I realized as time went on that this was the beginning of years of telling myself to suck it up and just feel lucky, years of feeling all the painful emotions for other people that I couldn't feel for myself. And I would feel very strong emotions for other people.

If I believed that something sad or scary or humiliating had happened in someone else's life, I felt those feelings deeply, sometimes more intensely than the person who I was empathizing with. Doesn't that qualify me as emotional?

***************1998****************

During my first counseling course, I realized that I approached class discussions strictly intellectually. In my estimation, people who responded emotionally weren't thinking clearly. I still had feelings, but I depersonalized them; I removed my emotions from my identity, the way I saw myself, because they clouded my thinking. I thought that was the mature way to handle emotions—until I read about how only people who are unhealthily detached from their emotions do that. I wondered if I might be detached from my emotions, but I didn't understand why that would be.

It was during that first counseling theories class in the summer that I was having coffee with my sister during a free moment in my busy schedule. It was before the final day when I got triggered, but I already was curious about my realization that I depersonalized my emotions. As our kids played in the next room I opened up about this self-discovery.

> "I don't directly voice my emotions. I don't say '*I feel sad*' or '*I feel scared*,'" I said to my sister.
>
> "What do you mean? You have emotions," she responded.
>
> "I know I do, but when I express them, it's kind of in a third-person way. I always say, 'It's a feeling of being sad,' or, 'It's a feeling of being scared.' I didn't realize I did that, or at least that it meant anything until I was reading that it's kind of a way to disown your feelings."
>
> "Why would you disown your feelings? I love examining my emotions."

My sister was emotional, I knew this. Immediately, I felt a bit superior for intellectualizing mine…then realized I had a long way to go.

Then, just months into my graduate program, I had my own psychologist. Amazing. I was already learning about what made people tick in my coursework, while also starting to discover what made *me* tick in therapy. I began to wonder if maybe I intellectualized my feelings because I didn't feel justified in having them. Admittedly, I couldn't figure out why I was still so bothered by this incident in my life when I never actually got hurt. It wasn't the awful situation that a lot of women experience, not like what my office colleague had gone through.

I brought this up to Rion. My constant need to understand the why of everything may have sometimes been a thorn in his side, but I appreciated the opportunity to internalize the knowledge that I was learning in my graduate classes—uncomfortably personal though it was. Rion explained,

> "Some experiences can cause disrupted memory storage. When some people are traumatized—by either one awful event or continued abuse—they just shove it away without thinking it through."
>
> "I worked with a woman who fought and was injured and raped," I said. "She was traumatized. I get that. And kids who suffer abuse throughout childhood are traumatized, and they survive by burying it. I get that too. But I didn't fight, I didn't flee. I just kind of froze. I actually tried to *appease* the guy by talking to him. Most of all, I didn't get hurt. Why do I have PTSD?"
>
> "Well, all the things you tried didn't save you," Rion replied. "You were raped. You were terrified, because you were at the mercy of a person you didn't know who threatened you and overpowered you."

"Yes. I thought he might kill me," I said. "But it's always bothered me that I didn't fight. I know I don't talk about my emotions. I always thought that made me strong, or at least tough. Then again, I also thought that him being convicted would be closure for me, and it wasn't."

"Well, the terror of that night stayed tucked away in your brain," Rion said. "You shoved it in that compartment where you stuff all the other things you haven't dealt with."

I thought to myself, *Along with my grandmother's death (and that humiliating date in college that I'm never going to talk about).*

At our next session, I asked Rion, "Why do I feel numb sometimes? I hate that feeling."

"Feeling numb is normal after an awful event," Rion replied. "It's too shocking to contemplate, so you don't. Before, when you tried to think about it, it didn't resolve itself, so you just stopped thinking and moved on."

"So I compartmentalized the feeling of being threatened, just like how I sometimes hide junk in my house I don't know what to do with? Everything that is out of place gets shoved out of sight—in the attic, in a drawer, in a box in the back of the closet. Usually, I don't think about that stuff again for years."

"That's one way to look at it," agrees Rion. "Then, as time goes on, more stuff gets shoved on top of what's already there. It gets so full you can't shove anything more in, and what is in there starts spilling out."

"But why am I feeling numb *now?*" I questioned. "It was a long time ago, I can't still be in shock."

"Those old feelings you stuffed away are coming out, now that we're talking about it. You are finally feeling the shock you didn't let yourself feel before."

Once I began this journey, I would periodically experience all sorts of unusual sensations. I might dissociate if I was in a situation that reminded me of something bad that had happened. For example, my husband and I once went on a drive in the country and passed a lovely meadow. Something about the dip in the road and the trees and the sunlight put me back to that college date, a time I'd rather forget. My husband kept talking, but my mind had taken a left turn. I didn't even hear him anymore. I was in a different world.

Nighttime shouldn't be full of ghosts and meadows should simply be beautiful places in the country. As much as I wanted to believe that stuffing my emotions away made me mature and healthy, I couldn't keep pretending that my unresolved trauma wasn't still affecting me. I couldn't hide from my past or my emotions any longer and maintain good mental health.

I had to clean up and organize my memories so they could be properly dealt with, then placed where they belonged and could be retrieved if I wanted. But it was a confusing mess. Everything was strewn everywhere. Just like overstuffed closets, that compartment in my brain had to be fully cleaned out before it could be organized and put back together. My feelings had to be combined with my story. I also needed to get rid of unrelated information that had gotten balled up with it all and had become triggers, like hilly roads through meadowlands. I couldn't do this on my own, though. Luckily, I had Rion there to help me.

But how does one find the right therapist in the first place? How did I go about finding Rion? Before journeying into the depths of therapy to overcome my PTSD, I should take a step back and talk about my realization that I needed to find a therapist.

It would be helpful to understand what seeking therapy entails.

THEME 2

THE
JOURNEY

L. FEIG KNIPE

CHAPTER 9

Seeking Therapy

"The only people who wouldn't benefit from going into therapy are the ones who are already in it." –My sister

In the late 70s, soon after college, I got a position as a social worker in Florida and worked there for several years before switching to the graphics company. In the late 80s, after my youngest son was born, I became a chapter director with the American Red Cross. As a helper, I have worked with people in my careers whose life decisions or fate put them in difficult circumstances. This sense of purpose was the call I felt to educate youth to make better life choices. I wanted to be a school counselor. This decision felt right. I loved the study, and the material was personal and interesting.

But this was only a small part of my life. It felt like I was living in multiple worlds.

It was summer 1998, and I was almost through my first counseling course. My three boys were full of energy and we lived in the country where they were always clambering for more adventure.

"Mom, can we go to the lake to go swimming?"
"Mom, can you take me into town?"
"Mom, when are you going to be done with that?"

I was spending every spare minute reading college textbooks or writing papers while trying to be available to them. I was doing my best to juggle it all, the big house and yard, my husband, the boys, the dog, my job, classes, and study.

But even in the midst of it all, my brain found the time and energy to focus on *that*.

I was in my car, in the parking lot of a supermarket. I was about to go into the store when suddenly I felt someone climbing on me.

"Why the hell am I thinking about this? Just stop!"

I knew it was not really happening, but I was experiencing the sensation and my mind wouldn't listen to me. It wouldn't move onto something else.

"Stop!"

But it wasn't stopping. I was in it, alone in my car. I was feeling it.

"Holy shit!" I yelled at myself. "What are you doing here, Linda? It's not 1980 anymore! You've decided to dwell on this after eighteen years? Just stop it! You've got stuff to do! Stop!"

It was not stopping.

I got out a little scrap of paper and deferred to my lifelong default for when I was overwhelmed by thoughts or feelings that bubbled up from the unknown. I started writing.

*He's crawling on top of me. Pushing me down. Hand over my
mouth,*

   *"Don't scream and you won't get hurt." I'm Scared...so
scared.*

I wrote what I was feeling. Finally it subsided. I was no
longer in it, but I chastised myself that I dwelled there at all. I
could control what I think—so why did I just take that perverse
little side trip down memory lane? Was I a drama queen wanting
to experience that? Was it being a drama queen to live in those
experiences by yourself, no audience required (Thank God)?

And then came my professor's statement about PTSD,

   *"Once symptoms surface, they won't be buried again. You can't
   just make them stop. You resolve it by working through it."*

I prayed, knowing that ultimately therapy was in the cards
for me—but I still argued about it with myself. As always, I
was keeping everything to myself, not talking to anyone. No
perspective but my own entered this discussion.

I don't need therapy—I just need to snap out of it, I admonished
myself.

   But, my professor said that was not going to happen, I
countered.

   I'm strong. I can take care of myself. My personal mantra.

   True, but what does that have to do with therapy?

   People will judge me if they know I'm in therapy? Now I was
getting into the weeds of my worries.

   Why do I think that?

   I really want to open up, but I don't want to.

   What is this about?

   Will my life change if I bring this out in the open? There it
was, the crux of my problem.

   What am I so scared will change?

What *was* I scared of? I did have skeletons in the closet. Would letting them out change the life I had built? The idea was paralyzing, so I didn't know the answer to that, but I couldn't stand the idea of anyone knowing my intimate secrets. I absolutely had no intention of talking about certain experiences, specifically that humiliating encounter on that date. But what if I slipped and revealed something?

It would feel good to talk though. To make that connection if I could just feel safe.

Some people, I think, have an inner wisdom telling them they need to talk to those they trust in order to make improvements in their lives. I'm not sure I had that voice, but I also don't think it would matter if I did, because I didn't think that my life needed to improve. I told myself that my life was good and I was lucky to have my family and my home. I just wanted the crazy stuff to stop. I didn't recognize at all that I might need to change myself. It certainly felt self-indulgent, paying someone to listen to me. It just seemed sad.

I did have a few people I could talk to. My close friend Grace was one. She was older, a true free spirit with a lot of kids and a nursing degree. She had experience, she was practical, and I trusted her advice. I knew she'd keep our conversations to herself. She was one of 'my people.'

> "Honestly, I just worry about the stigma. What if people find out?"
>
> Grace countered, "No one is going to know you're in therapy, you know. You are the only one who can tell them, so that is in your control. Besides, plenty of people have been in therapy. It's just your perception that anyone would even care."

"I don't know if I even want to go," I continued, shifting tactics. "I don't really like talking about myself. They'll probably ask me a whole bunch of hard questions…"

"You only share what you are comfortable sharing," she said. "You do not have to answer people's questions if you don't want to. Though, therapy does require vulnerability and you're pretty guarded. Maybe that's something you can work on with a therapist."

"Well…how do I even pay for it?"

"You call anyone in the mental health field and ask. I know you have insurance, but I also know people can go to the local Mental Health Office at Social Services or a lot of agencies out there. Any of them can tell you who you should look for and how to pay. There are options for most everyone."

The conversation with Grace helped, but I kept thinking up other roadblocks, like how I was even going to fit this in. I had so much going on in my life. Could I even find time for appointments?

I said to Grace, "One of the reasons I don't like to talk is there's so much craziness swirling around in my head it will take years to explain it. And what if this therapist doesn't work out? I would have to start all over again to try to explain it to someone new!"

"Maybe," Grace replied. "But, while it feels like a lot of craziness in your head, the right therapist can focus on the right pieces of information pretty quickly to get somewhere."

Finally I visited my doctor, who immediately noticed my disturbed demeanor.

"You've been feeling down for a while. How are you doing now?"

"I'm not feeling very well. About anything. A conversation in my counseling class made me start to remember a time I was assaulted…raped," I replied. "I'm looking for a therapist now."

"Are you depressed?"

"Nothing I haven't dealt with before. I was told by my professor that I likely have PTSD."

"I'm glad you are interested in starting therapy. It's a journey, but eventually, you're going to be fine again."

"Eventually! I was hoping this would only take a little while! How long does it take to get over PTSD?"

My doctor realized I wasn't ready to talk about this journey. He said, "You are also struggling with depression. You've got a lot going on in your life."

"I'm strong," I repeated my mantra.

"Yes, but even strong people get sick." Then he continued more quietly, "When I was in medical school I suffered from severe depression on and off while I was there. My college roommates were so concerned about me they took me to the clinic and I was hospitalized. It's been a battle all my life, but I've gotten help. Help is what you are getting for yourself now."

My doctor, an extraordinarily kind and accomplished physician, researcher, author, and speaker, also felt the weight of his world and of being a strong helper. He was comparing his situation to mine. It helped me tremendously, taking away some of the loneliness and shame I was feeling.

"If you think of depression like being sick, like having caught something that you need treatment for, it might be easier to accept treatment."

I admired this man who had just revealed some of his own struggles to me. It helped me as I resolved to do everything necessary to make myself better.

So, after all the questioning, talking, and ruminating, I said to myself, "I'll get therapy for that break-in and rape." But deep down, I knew there were things I would never talk about.

I wanted to find a therapist with a specialty in trauma, based on discussions we had in class about treating PTSD. Finding a male therapist mattered to me, too, although I'm not sure why. I think I felt more protected taking this scary journey with a man. I read once that when children want to be nurtured they want their mothers, but when they are hurt or scared they want their fathers. I later realized I have a perception of men as fixers (I once said to Rion in exasperation, "I just want you to fix this!")

One major problem was the discomfort I was feeling at the thought of creating visualizations about my body. I kept this to myself because I couldn't really put my finger on why this worried me so much. Over time, I realized I had a strong need to control how others saw me, how they thought of me, which was a big part of it. However, despite my worries, I also knew if I didn't talk to a professional, the only perspective I would have was my own, and frankly that wasn't helping. I was told I could heal and I believed it. I just had to be brave.

I looked in the city directory where I was attending graduate college classes. I reached out and had callbacks from several clinical psychologists who answered my questions over the phone. When I talked with Rion, who eventually became my therapist, he told me what I could expect. He suggested I come for an appointment and then decide if we should work together

CHAPTER 10

Starting Therapy

"Therapy is just to help you understand yourself better. If you choose to make changes after that it's up to you, but at least you'll be in a better position to evaluate yourself if you are honest with yourself and understand where stuff comes from." –Grace

That summer of 1998, as I was struggling with this new problem of mine, my son was being tutored in the nearby city where I was attending my college classes. After leaving him with the tutor, I had an hour to myself so I headed to the psychologist's office just up the street. Upon entering the waiting room, a little window opened and I was greeted by a very stern-looking receptionist. She had the demeanor of a well seasoned guard with little use for people who didn't know or follow the rules. She told me I could make an appointment to see the psychologist, but there was no way I was going to talk to him right then. He was in session with no time between appointments. I was very uncomfortable. I made an appointment—his earliest was three weeks out—and I left. I didn't know if this guy was going to feel okay to talk to, but I was quite sure I didn't want to misstep around her again.

Three weeks later, in the final days of August, I had my first therapy appointment.

When I first met Dr. Kweller, I had a lot of trepidation. I didn't know what to expect. I was looking forward to being able to talk, but I was dreading talking. This was actually the first time I talked to him about my trauma. This appointment was the actual beginning of my healing journey.

He started with, "Tell me about yourself."

I should have been ready for this.

"Well, I'm married. I have three boys, ages nine to fourteen. I'm in graduate school to be a school counselor, and I work full time in our high school counseling office so I'm very busy. I'm not sure what else to tell you."

I smiled. I wanted to make a good impression, to show I was mentally healthy (hah) and let him know I was a strong person.

"You have a lot going on. What brings you in here?"

Here we go...

"Oh, well, I was, (pause) assaulted a long time ago and for some reason I can't stop thinking about it right now. It's making it really difficult for me to do anything and I have so much to do. I just keep having flashbacks, or having nightmares about ghosts, or people chasing me, or waking up and not being able to sleep. I haven't been able to eat. That's not normal," I said with a self-deprecating smile.

I imagined what I must've looked like to him. I was an overweight, middle-aged woman, complaining about her dreams. I actually didn't even know what I looked like. I've always thought about appearance. I would see myself in the mirror, but I couldn't tell if I looked as big to other people as I did to myself. I'd have liked to control how others saw me. I worried how people saw me, what they were thinking about me—like, all the time. I couldn't hide that I'm nearly six feet tall and not thin. I used to be. I wanted to be. I was in my early forties but I felt matronly. I figured he must've thought I was so weak to be overweight like this. My remarks about food were a defense before he said it first.

> "I just need to get control of my mind," I continued, determined to come off as professional, serious. "I don't know how to do that. I just keep telling myself to stop thinking about it, but I can't. Not being able to control my thoughts is driving me crazy."
>
> "Can you tell me what happened?" He was being quiet and very neutral with his tone. My nervousness was calming a bit.
>
> "Uh, a guy came into my apartment in the middle of the night. This was nearly twenty years ago, now, um in 1980. I was just twenty-five and living in my own apartment for the first time. I woke up and he was standing next to my bed. He got on top of me and he assaulted me and he left. I called my boss and they came and took me to the hospital. The hospital called the police."
>
> "Do you mean he sexually assaulted you?"
>
> "Yes."
>
> "Was there penetration? Did he rape you?"
>
> (God, I hate those words.) "Yes."

This was the beginning of the 'get to know you' phase of therapy. I wasn't really sure how I felt about this person, how much I wanted to tell him, or how helpful he could be.

I wasn't bold enough to dart out of there, but I was uncomfortable enough that I didn't know if I would come back.

He continued his questions:

"What did you think when you woke up and there was someone standing next to your bed?"

"Well, first, I thought it was Brian, the husband of my friend who lives down the street. He had medical issues before that put him in the hospital, and his wife was away on a business trip. I thought for a second he was having medical problems again and he needed my help."

"But it wasn't him?"

"No, I didn't know who it was."

"Can you talk about that?"

"Well, I started to scream and he put his hand over my mouth and told me not to scream and he wouldn't hurt me. Then he…he got on me." This was hard for me to say, I was feeling very exposed. "I was thinking I need to just pretend this is someone I know, wait until he's gone. I don't remember thinking about anything else. I kept talking to him partly because he was trying to kiss me and I didn't want him to so if he was talking, he wouldn't kiss me. I also was thinking maybe I could connect with him a bit so he wouldn't want to hurt me."

"How did you feel when you realized what was happening?"

My body was buzzing when the therapist asked me these questions and more so as I thought about how to answer. I didn't understand the feeling, but it felt like electricity running through my veins, very uncomfortable, like I'd just been shocked.

"Well, I guess I thought he might hurt me."

"How did you feel about that?"

"Um, I didn't want it to happen."

"Can you tell me how that felt?"

(The buzzing is getting worse.)

I don't understand what this guy is asking me. I keep telling him what I was thinking, but that doesn't seem to be what he's looking for.

I started wringing my hands.

How long before this is over? This is very uncomfortable
So I asked, "What do you mean? I told you."

"You told me what you were thinking. I was wondering what you were feeling." His reply left me in a quandary I wasn't aware of before. There's a difference between saying how you think and how you feel? *Well, of course there is! So why couldn't I do it?*

I realized it was helpful to know what was working well in my life and what was missing. I didn't know, until that moment, that I was missing emotions—and that was a bad thing. I thought being more intellectual in my approach was a choice, a good one. I continued the dialogue about emotions, as best I could.

"I guess there was definitely a scared feeling. I think maybe there was a feeling of disgust. He smelled like beer and cigarettes. I don't know."

"So you were scared and you were disgusted. Is that how you felt?"

"Yeah, I guess."

"Thank you for sharing that with me. I know you want to be able to control what you're thinking about."

Would this strangely uncomfortable dialogue we just had help me control my thinking? The doctor made a quick note and looked at me to be sure my attention was still with him. He started to explain what I was experiencing.

"You are suffering from Post Traumatic Stress Disorder. PTSD. You may have heard of Shell Shock, a term that was used in the past for combat veterans who came back after fighting, and were re-experiencing the combat situations. That was also PTSD. It happens to some people after life-threatening events. We can work through this, but it's going to take some time before those thoughts and feelings go away."

So I was going to have to add therapy to my schedule.

"Talking about it will help?"

"Did you notice we went through your experience with the rape several times just now? The first time you just told me what happened. The second time you told me what you thought about it. The third time we actually started to talk about how you felt about it. That's where healing can actually happen. This kind of talking is called Cognitive Behavior Therapy. Eventually, if we keep sorting through your thoughts and feelings about everything that happened, you'll be able to put it all together, sort out your feelings, and file it away in your memory the way it's supposed to be, rather than the tangled confusion it is now. Then, it won't keep popping up and bothering you."

Well, that's what I wanted, for it to stop bothering me, but the word 'eventually' was a bit off putting. How long was this therapy going to take? I had a lot going on in my head as he asked:

"Do you want to keep working on this with me? Should we make another appointment?"

There weren't enough hours in the day. I was already away from my family two or three nights a week and felt like I was walking on eggshells around my husband. Money was tight. I was working long hours. But if this is what it took to fix myself, then ...

"Well, I guess I have to," I said. "Yes."

Being brave enough to start over with therapy again felt like a huge undertaking. Revealing secrets to a therapist and ultimately to myself would bring about full self-awareness, and with the right person, we were talking about the important stuff immediately. I knew I had found my therapist because I felt acknowledged and validated.

CHAPTER 11

Pursuing Therapy

It had been a week. The kids and I had just started back to school and I was also in my second week of classes at college. The grant program I worked through would run out in two years. If I wanted to keep working in the schools I'd need a Masters Degree in Education and then hope to be hired. I had already finished two graduate courses in Counselor Education but the PTSD symptoms made everything extremely stressful. My oldest son was a freshman in high school and in the school's competitive marching band as well as soccer. We were on the run constantly. Was I really going to add therapy appointments to my already packed schedule?

Yes, I had to.

I had little time to myself and was anxious about talking, but I couldn't wait to talk. I'd been wanting to talk forever.

A week after my first session, I was again at my psychologist's office. He introduced himself when we first met as Dr. Kweller. I wondered if that's how he wanted to be addressed, but he said his first name was Rion and I could use whatever name I preferred. I thought about this all week. I decided because he called me by my first name, I would call him Rion.

He was wearing the professional man's uniform, a business suit. He looked fit and perfectly pulled together. *How in the world do you stay in shape just sitting and talking all day?* He offered me coffee as we went into the inner sanctum of his office. *I'd love to drink coffee and talk all day, but I certainly don't look fit and put together like he does.* I had seen some of the other therapists in the practice as they came to greet their clients in the waiting room. I guessed I looked a little more like them. While I tried to pull off 'attractive,' there was my overweight issue and 'business casual' really wasn't the look I preferred. I was always self-conscious about my appearance. It didn't help my anxiety about all of this …

"How have you been this past week? How did you feel after we first talked?"

Oh, shit—we're talking now. It means I'm talking.

"Oh, I guess it felt good to be able to say what was going on with me. Things are so busy in my life with my kids, my work, and my grad program, I guess I'm not really sure how I felt about it."

(Liar, liar, pants on fire. You did nothing but think about this all week. You had feelings about it, too, but there are no words for that. What did I FEEL? What DID I feel?) My thoughts were not aligning with the words I was sharing with Rion.

"Okay," he responds. Then, silence.

He's not talking! What the hell?

"Um, I'm not sure how all this works." Maybe I could get him to explain things to me so I'd know how I should respond, what I should talk about. I couldn't start. I couldn't pick what we were going to talk about. That would be too revealing. That would give a clue about what I spent my time thinking about, then I would be open to being judged. He might think I had mental health problems, or I was weak, or what I worried about was trivial, boring, not worth his time. I couldn't let myself be vulnerable. If I perceived he thought less of me by what I said, it would hurt too much. I wouldn't risk it.

"I'm here for you to talk about whatever you need to talk about. You can talk about anything you want. You're in control."

Shit, shit, shit. I can't just start talking. I can't even think of what to say. The rape isn't bothering me at all when I'm sitting here, so what am I supposed to be talking about?

This conundrum was an issue for me throughout my time in therapy. I was there because I had been raped long ago, and it obviously had started affecting me, but it wasn't front and center in my mind. Problems at home more often occupied my conscious thoughts. Issues related to the rape would come out at odd times when I was alone, but be buried again when I went to therapy, so I often didn't know what to talk about.

"I guess I'm so busy I can't just pick something to talk about. There's so much." *Linda, you're an idiot. If there's so much, just pick something. You're pathetic.*

He waited patiently.

Eventually, I added, "Umm—my husband is mad at me."

"What's going on with your husband?"

"He says I'm not taking care of the boys or him. He says I'm away a lot and when I'm home, I'm still not available. He says he has to earn all the money and take care of the boys and the house and shopping and even dinner. He does do all those things, but I do too. He said I needed help, but now that I'm getting help he's mad that I'm coming here—taking more time away. He thinks I just need to stop thinking about myself all the time and think more about all of them. He doesn't see everything I'm trying to do to make our life better or to make myself better."

"Do both you and your husband work full time?" Rion started to help me talk.

"Well, yes, though I don't work when school is out. Just college classes. He earns most of the money though. I don't make as much right now."

"Is it unusual that your husband is mad at you? Would you call your marriage healthy?"

"Oh, my husband loves me. We love each other. Our boys are great. We actually have a good marriage."

"Okay."

Silence.

"I guess I'm having a hard time sleeping...or staying asleep. I don't know what to do with everything I've got going on and all the thoughts. After I left here last time I just kept thinking about what we talked about. I have a hard time going to sleep, then it wakes me up and I think some more. I'm not sleeping very much."

Okay, I picked the topic. Now he can talk.

"We talked about a number of things. What was bothering you when you were trying to sleep?"

"Well, the assault stuff I guess...um, the rape. I can't get it out of my mind."

"Can you talk a bit about what you can't stop thinking about?"

This conversation did not flow easily. There were long silences in between much of our dialogue. Rion was silently insisting I take the lead and I was silently resisting. Finally I was able to land on something to say.

"It was just so gross. Details keep popping up like I'm feeling them. How scary it was when I woke up and he was standing next to my bed. Him..." (I always struggle to say, 'getting on me.' It's too much.) "The cigarette and beer smell. It was all gross. I keep feeling how gross it was."

We lingered a bit in this memory. Rion gently prompted me to go further into my experience; what I thought, what I did, and more importantly, how I felt.

> "You were scared and you've said a number of times it was so gross."
> "Oh my God. Yes. It was like having a slug on me."

I immediately recoiled from that mental image, which I felt with my entire body. Rion could see my revulsion and pulled me back to the present. Sometimes digging up memories from PTSD involved trying to avoid landmines that would start the re-experiencing. It was a delicate operation.

> Finally, he said, "That sounds awful. You've shared a very difficult experience with me. What are you feeling now?"
> "Um, I'm not sure. I feel nauseous. It's hard to start talking and it feels pretty distasteful to talk about that stuff...to go there. It's a really offensive feeling."

I'm symbolically unscrewing and screwing on the cap of my water bottle as I talk: open up, close up. I feel that buzzy feeling. I'm uncomfortable.

> "I don't know how I'm going to do everything I have to do with so little sleep."
> "There are things you can do to put all those thoughts someplace. You can meditate, or pray, or talk to someone, get some exercise. You can write."
> "I've been writing and praying."
> "Good. Keep at it and we'll talk more about this next time we meet. Can we put a few appointments on the calendar?"
> "I guess that would be good to get appointments that fit my schedule better."

"Good. Thank you for trusting me. We'll talk more about all those flashbacks as we keep meeting. We will keep working through them until they don't bother you."

He stood, the signal that time was up.

Already? I checked the clock—shit, was I really in there for forty-five minutes? I felt uncomfortable and buzzy as I left his office. Getting started talking about stuff was like pulling teeth—a long, painful process. So many silences as time slowly stretched on. Then I would barely figure out what I was going to say, finally start talking and it was time to go. Damn it.

So I figured out, after two sessions with Rion, that I focused on my thoughts and excluded emotions to avoid pain. While I was in my therapy sessions, I could talk about being raped and other issues that impacted my life, but I struggled with discussing the parts I didn't want to say aloud.

Describing my feelings was something I'd not done for a long time, but the re-experiencing required that I go there. If I wanted to get better, I had to connect to those emotions I'd shoved in a closet so long ago.

Therapist Notes September '98*

9/17/98   **Linda**   **Individual Session**

Patient "agitated"

"Moderate to extreme discomfort"

Says not anxiety

Needs to cry deep down—didn't let self cry

Full of shame and guilt. No eye contact.

Hand over face. Could not tell husband that the rape affected the way she responded to him. Faked it. Didn't explain disinterest

---

9/24/98   **Linda**   **Individual Session**

Sleeping better, feeling better

Still significantly blocked from feelings

Afraid of damaging marriage

Afraid of upsetting status quo

Needed to get up from chair and stand at window way across the room

Diagnosis: PTSD with Depression

Plan: Same CBT (Cognitive Behavioral Therapy)
RB Kweller, Ph.D

* *My therapist shared copies of some of his notes with me when I told him I was writing about my experience of therapy. He told me the notes are mine to use as I wish. All language is his.*

CHAPTER 12

Journal Honesty

I began a journal as soon as I started therapy. I wrote constantly during those first three years. It helped, even writing on scraps of paper if I was without my journal. I had always written my feelings when I felt overwhelmed, I do to this day, so I started writing notes about the confusing sensations that had begun even before I met Rion. Much of my therapy involved perspective shifts and realizations that occurred as I wrote. They highlighted my thoughts and experiences of therapy as well as shifts in thinking that would help precipitate healing.

But still, I kept trying to do therapy right, so I didn't talk about things that were affecting me in ways I didn't understand. If it didn't have to do with the rape I wouldn't bring it up, even when I should have. Time was wasted as Rion tried to get me to take control of my session and talk about anything of significance. I wanted him to be in charge, to ask questions and fix me. But how was he supposed to know how to do that without my participation? It was like a big investigation with me hiding information.

I had talked about shoving things in the closet that I couldn't deal with, but there was also a wall in front of my mind's eye. Not all the time, but sometimes, we would be talking and something would be said or remembered—and bam! There was the wall, and I couldn't talk anymore. Memories were just below the surface, but unreachable. I would leave therapy, shaken, and it would take until nighttime for those memories to finally begin breaking through.

Then my journals were the avenue for discovery...

I need strategies. But how do I talk about something that feels nearly impossible to talk about? I want someone to ask the right questions to get me over the hump, but that will never work, so what can I do to open myself up? Can I be so brave to say I need to talk about the rape? I need to feel things? This is so screwed up. I can talk about being assaulted, if somehow it comes up related to what else we're talking about.

But, there's so much more to it and then I get in there with Rion and I'm not thinking about that at all. I'm thinking about the shit that goes on in my regular life. The assault... the rape only comes out when I'm alone or in the middle of the night. It's what eats at me and makes me feel crazy, but it's not in my mind when I have the chance to talk about it.

I wish Rion would ask questions, but he won't make me talk about anything I don't choose. It's a conundrum. I wish I could just talk once, put it out there, and be better, but I guess that's not how it works. I guess I have to be able to keep talking about it and find all the hidden parts that are making me crazy. I hope then I can be done with this. I hope I can make myself talk more. I need to talk.

I'm just feeling so isolated. And where do I start? And do I have to go through it all? I didn't really say much about the trial, I just think about it. That was hard too. So it was all hard and remembering it is so difficult. How am I supposed to walk into that office and work up the courage to start it up myself? It's like I'm initiating an assault on myself every week.

But I don't know how to go back and talk about anything if I don't feel anything—if that wall goes up and I can't talk or feel or think. When I go into his office and Rion waits for me to start on an issue ... I don't know if he realizes that my inability to do so is the issue, it's the reason therapy was so necessary. My inability to talk about issues of importance to me is the most important, the biggest problem I have. The assault is only the foot in the door to my problems.

It's not just the rape. I can't talk about any difficult issues, like my relationships with my children and my husband. I start, but shut down too quickly. And then, when I talk about the rape, it doesn't feel like it's in the past. I experience shock and fear whenever I talk about it, and that affects me for days.

Now I've begun experiencing something new since we started pulling out the memories.

I continued writing:

I got the creeps really badly. I was trying to identify the feeling, and I got incapacitated. I couldn't drive for at least fifteen minutes. I was sitting in the car with the creeps. What is the feeling? Standing with your back to a wall full of spiders and snakes behind you and over your head. That's the creeps. But no identifiable emotions or thoughts attached, just horrible cringing and shivering in your back and throughout your body. It's worse in my back. A really uncomfortable, crawl-out-of-your-skin feeling.

I told Rion.

"It feels like bugs are behind me. It's a very creepy feeling. I don't know what that's about."

"Does it feel like that all the time?"

"No, just at the oddest times. I was out alone in a crowd the other night, not with people I knew, and it started. A creepy feeling. I don't know what to make of it."

"Huh. That's interesting," was Rion's non-explanation.

I couldn't figure out what was causing that feeling for the longest time, until I finally made the connection as I was writing again...

... 'the creeps' is the feeling you get when you're sitting around the campfire and everyone is telling really scary stories and you want to look behind you, but you're embarrassed the others might laugh at you. So your back gets a cold, Heebie Jeebies kind of shuddering fear...

"I think I understand that creepy feeling now," I told Rion.

"Really? What do you think it is?"

"...It's fear of what's about to happen. 'The creeps' are dread. I'm feeling dread."

Suddenly, I recognized an actual feeling. I had felt dread when I was raped, but I stuffed that away until the sensation started coming out in therapy. I had felt dread when I woke to find a shadowy figure next to my bed, and the dread continued as I waited for him to be done and then get rid of me.

Putting a name to the sensation felt kind of amazing. I was beginning to understand what this journey was about: putting words to feelings to make meaning of my experience. And it was extraordinary to be sitting in the patient chair, getting an insider's view of therapy as I was learning about it in counseling classes.

"You just named an emotion," Rion said. "That's good work."

I thought a lot about my therapy experience and about how hard it was. In class, my professors would talk about unconditional positive regard, that whatever one reveals, one should feel positive regard from the therapist, without condition. I didn't view myself with positive regard, however. I only seemed to feel that when I talked to God.

Talking to God was easy because God already knew me. Unlike Rion or anyone else, I also didn't have to look into God's eyes as I spoke or worry about the look or comments I might get. God, for me, was accepting. God loves me and as hard as some things were, I believed this, then as now. I know it.

I wondered how much time I wasted worrying about what my therapist thought of me? How much further along would I have been if I talked to him plainly, like I talked to God?

As time went by I started to consider that God put me together with Rion for a reason. I started to think that when I hid myself and thought I was being strong and self-sufficient, I was skirting God's plan that we are to help one another. I realized that we are not meant to do life on our own. We are social animals. But I needed to feel safe and nurtured when going into the yucky stuff that was so hard for me to look at. As Rion and I journeyed there together, with his positive regard, I gained a new and valuable perspective. It helped me let go of some of the harsh judgements I had carried about myself. From what I was learning in my counseling classes and my own experience, I realized this was familiar territory for a therapist.

What Rion was actually thinking about me was how to help me. I had to learn to let him.

I pondered all this in my journals. I could start to see not only the dawning of understanding, but the early emergence of some emotions in my journals and in talking to God.

I knew back then, after it happened, that I needed to talk about it all, over and over, to get it out. But no one wanted to talk with me, they would skirt it, talk about anything else. So it got put away. But I wanted to talk, I still do. I don't think Rion understands that I want to talk, he sees me struggling and is very careful. There are feelings here that I never knew and I'm starting to get mad now, but then it's all back into the drawer. I can feel the drawer sliding shut. Everything is folded down tight, my face and emotions clear, it's deep in me again. Put away. But my chest is starting to hurt now. That scares me.

A question for Rion about the process: If I'm talking about something and feeling it and then shutting down, why doesn't he keep me on the subject and the thoughts? Is he being careful? Is it something I have to learn to stay with myself? It bottles me up when I put it away.

I continued to talk to my journal every night.

Questions, questions, millions of questions. There isn't anything for me to grab onto. I am not getting information so I have no starting point. I have bits and pieces of information that aren't always accurate because they're just my suppositions, so I cannot process them. There are so many holes, I just shut down.

Let me connect my feelings to my thoughts!

I need information, let me pick your brain, Rion. What do you think is wrong, a problem for me? Is it common? What are the causes? What are your goals for me? I have two: my husband and the rape. What are you writing on the insurance forms? Condition? Diagnosis?

I wish I were brave enough to ask. I don't know why I don't ask when I write him letters. I just explain how I'm feeling so he understands, but I'm afraid to ask for stuff. I don't know why that is. I need to start writing topics to bring up in therapy, then I'll remember to say it.

Rion had demonstrated his ability to help me, to let me be in control, to not judge me and to keep my confidence. But if I didn't think that he could be 100 percent trustworthy all the time, I didn't trust him at all. I could either tell him all my deep, dark secrets, or I couldn't tell him anything at all. Black and white thinking is all or nothing and my black and white thinking made it difficult to progress. I wanted information from him so I could figure out the answers, but I was the one who was keeping information he needed tucked away from him in the drawers and closets of my mind. I wanted to control what he thought or visualized about me. Continuing like this gave Rion little chance of earning my trust enough to help me.

Life and everything in it is nuanced, like a whole spectrum of colors. But still, I let black and white thinking interfere with my therapy for quite a while. I was resisting learning to initiate our conversations in therapy and then leaving angry that Rion didn't take the lead when I knew that's not how it worked.

> *I don't know why he can't ask me a damn question if I tell him I want him to. I just want to get this all out in the open so I can be done with it. But he just lets me pick around the edges at stuff and it isn't getting me very far.*
>
> *If I can't get anywhere faster I just want to stop.*
>
> *But I can't stop. I can't keep living with this craziness in my head.*

I was slowly coming to terms with the idea that I was going to have to rely on hope, faith, and trust. Hope that I would get better. Faith in Rion, as he offered me the unconditional positive regard that I needed and trust in the process, which I continued to work on. I hoped trust would come in time. I realized through journaling that I needed to be patient as I was getting rid of the toxins in my body. The emotions that I should have felt eighteen years before were now coming to the surface. I just needed to stick it out.

By this point, I knew I needed to talk about my emotions—but the words that describe emotions were elusive for me. For quite a long time I was unable to comprehend Rion's explanations, either of what was happening to me or where I was headed in therapy. He knew how to help me reawaken my emotional self and when I asked, he would explain it to me. I would almost grasp what he was talking about until I walked out the door of his office and his explanation would be lost again. I used to liken it to almost grasping a difficult math concept in class when I was a student, but then when I was trying to use what I had learned for my homework that night, my understanding had slipped away. I was a cognitive thinker who understood concepts and I thought that included emotions. What I thought, however, and the sensations I felt, didn't sync up.

Rion frequently said that for good mental health I needed to connect to my emotions. Mental health was a term that caused me grief. I was bothered a lot that Rion would talk about improving my mental health. I interpreted this as him saying I was mentally ill, and I took great offense, which I told him repeatedly.

Just for the record, looking back, I would agree. I was mentally ill.

CHAPTER 13

Trust

Trust can be a challenge for those of us in therapy. It's also a requirement for therapy to be effective. I had been in therapy for just a month when I had an exchange with Rion about trust. We were proceeding in fits and starts. I still resisted bringing up topics for us to discuss.

******************1998**********************

"If we are going to make progress here in therapy, you will have to decide to trust me," he stated.

I was a bit taken aback by his assertion so I did what I usually do: try to give people what they're looking for. Rion was looking for trust, so I told him, "I trust you."

"Right," he drolly agreed.

I did think I trusted him, until I mulled it over more deeply during the following week. I started to feel conflicted about the idea that I should trust someone I didn't really know, a person I'd only met a month ago. I got annoyed by just the thought of it, then I got angry. The more I tried to resolve my issue with trust, the more stuck I felt. I wrote extensively over a period of time about the struggle of understanding what it really means to trust someone.

I started to research definitions of trust. There were a lot that reinforced my feelings that I was justified in not trusting my therapist.

Trust implies an assured attitude toward another which may rest on evidence from experience and more subjective grounds such as knowledge, affection, admiration, respect or reverence. Definitions from Webster's Unabridged Dictionary[3] says:

> *Trust* is "a charge or duty imposed in faith or confidence or as a condition of some relationship."
> *Trust* is "a person, or thing in which confidence is placed."
> *Trust* is "the obligation...of one to whom something is confided."

I had to figure this trust thing out. I wrote constantly in my journal and in letters that I never sent to Rion:

> *I am afraid about therapy. I know dread describes the assault, the rape—there's a haunting, shuddering fear that I yearn to escape. I am desperate—in extreme danger—I could die soon— how? Will it hurt? Will I linger? Will I be choking—trying to breathe while I leave this life? Dread and desperation—no wonder I've hidden.*
> *Hide.*
> *I feel more than nervous, more than agitated. Anguish— extreme torment. It's been days of turmoil. Trying to reconcile trust—my need to trust and my inability to trust. Why should I? I'm vacillating between hopelessness and despair and anger over this. I need to escape. This is too much. I am so angry at Kweller for suggesting I trust him. I don't even know him, it's manipulative. The mindfuck I was scared of.*

The definitions in the dictionary reinforced my apprehension.

I continued to write about my struggle to trust in my journal, the only place where my emotions had free reign. Then I had a flashback from the rape:

I feel it. Hands grabbing my face and neck. Struggle. What am I imagining this for? That didn't happen! Why am I making this part of it up? I know what happened. Now I'm pretending it was scarier than I thought? Or do I think suddenly there's a part I don't remember. I know I remember everything. So why am I making that up? It's awful. I feel it.

After sitting with the memory and the feelings, I knew.

It did happen! That's how I woke up. I didn't forget it, it was never significant before. I didn't get choked, but his hands were over my mouth, near my throat. I was so afraid of being choked. What did he say?

"I won't hurt you. Stop screaming and I won't hurt you!" He might as well have said, 'Trust me.'

I've heard 'trust me' before in my life. Guys who pretend they care about you... who end up dumping you... or worse.

If you hear, 'Trust me,' beware.

In my life, I've been through the cycle of getting emotionally involved, trusting, caring, passion, uncertain, then dumped many times, and sometimes physically hurt. I had to think this through and figure it out. After all my ruminating in my journals, I realized it must be a perspective question, so I addressed it more academically.

What do I know? I know I don't trust. What is my perspective about trust? I have no basis to trust. The question: Is this an accurate perception or am I being irrational?

Writing in my journal later that night, this memory surfaced ...

'Who is in my room? Oh, it's my friend from next door needing help. Is he sick again—what's wrong?'

Danger! You trusted wrong! Hands on face, neck, fear, disbelief.

I don't trust myself to pick what to trust.

With this realization I stopped writing—such a clear memory. I didn't trust *myself*.

How could I not see that? I felt gullible in relationships. I wanted to trust so much sometimes but it wasn't always safe to do so. As I thought about therapy, I wrote in my journal:

I want to trust Rion.

Rion has a duty to me as my therapist. I can entrust my secrets, fears, thoughts, emotions with him to be cared for. He has an obligation to keep my confidence and understand and help me if I share my thoughts and feelings with him.

As I read further in the extensive examples that my dictionary provided, I saw this description.

People fail in their trust, but they live up to it far more often (5b, reference Boy Scout handbook).[4]

I could accept this explanation of trust.

I will give up control here, I will let Rion help me.

I will have faith.

Definition: Faith is "a firm or unquestioning belief in something for which there is no proof."[5]

My realization:

Faith—I control.

Trust—control is out of my hands. I have to give up control.

Definitions started to occupy my journals. Defining trust and faith started my period of defining words related to feelings and behavior. It may seem strange, but at that time in my therapy, I kept Webster's Third New International Dictionary (1971st ed) close at hand. It was my way of moving from my cognitive approach toward everything to identifying the feelings that should go along with my thoughts. Having emotions be described concretely really helped me to start attaching those feelings to my memories and thoughts. It was helpful to take words that are nuanced and to be very clear about the meaning they convey. To look at and understand what I was unpacking from the closet was a big step forward in my healing. I had pages of definitions from my journals and I still look up definitions online to this day, which helps me to understand and convey my emotions.

CHAPTER 14

Outside Influences

Life

In the years leading up to my struggles with PTSD and mental health issues, my husband and I built a house that should have been within our means. In the decade since we married, he had socked away a significant amount of money since becoming an insurance agent. He was rewarded along the way with a good income and regular family trips that he won for all of us to attend conferences.

In early 1994, the boys were still at an age to be content in the bosom of the family. It was exciting to finally be living our dream in a country home with land for our kids to play on and woods with a stream out back. It was before they realized how far outside of the village and their friends they actually were. My husband was successful and I was proud of him. We made financial commitments to our new home and for the first few years after we moved in things were going well. Our financial obligations with our new home contributed to my own career decision later that same year and I got a grant funded full-time job at the local public school. Then over the next few years, problems began to arise in his professional world.

In 1998, the year when it seemed all our troubles collided, he informed me we had a problem with our finances. I responded to him by exclaiming,

> "I don't understand. What do you mean, 'Our income is a lot lower than you expected'?"
>
> "The company lied to me. My managers have told me over the years that I would be vested after ten years and get the renewals from all the policies and other business that I have already sold. Now suddenly they're saying that I will only get renewals from what I sell from ten years going forward. That's around $100,000 of money that I was expecting that they say we're not going to get!"

I was shocked and my husband was livid and near tears as he talked. An attorney had advised that all the agents who had been misled might be able to go up against the company, however, it was a huge insurance company with deep pockets. There was not much chance of recouping the loss. It would be better to simply move on rather than spend years and more money fighting them.

> "What are you going to do? You can't quit, we have our home we have to pay for!" My desperation left little room for the sympathetic ear my husband needed.
>
> He replied in defeat, "I don't know how I can keep working for them knowing that they lie. I can't trust anything they tell me."

****************1998******************

Therapy

In my therapist's office, I kept going back and forth about how we got to this point, all the factors contributing to my troubles, trying to sort through it for Rion, and maybe more for myself.

> "My husband, along with a lot of other agents, are going to jump ship. Our income is nothing close to what he had been promised."
>
> "I've been hearing this from other agents who are patients of mine. It's a huge betrayal. I can understand your husband's anger," Rion commented.

I was relieved that he understood and especially that this truly was an issue of this company lying to their agents and not just my husband's misunderstanding.

> "Well, we have debt and huge monthly payments. Our house isn't extravagant, but it's our home. We love it. We have to try to save it." I continued, "My husband is looking for a new job."
>
> "And what about you?" Rion inquired. "You said you are working and attending graduate classes?"
>
> "Yes. I'm working full-time while the boys are all in school. But it's just a grant-funded position in the counseling department. We need a lot more than it pays, so I hope to get hired as a school counselor as soon as I have my degree. If I go year round, I can get my master's degree in two years, which is right when the grant runs out."

Talking to a therapist was helpful. I wasn't sleeping, couldn't eat, struggled with study, and was barely functioning for my family. And financially, things were difficult but spending so much time getting him up to speed so he understood my world was intimidating. I just wanted to get over the PTSD craziness.

My husband was in his own world of hurt. The betrayal by his company brought back issues of childhood mistreatment that were traumatic for him. Much of his distrust was transferred to me. I had always described our marriage as loving but volatile—the bottom line is we were a mismatched couple having marital problems, exacerbated by trauma and emotional issues on both sides.

To help with our finances, instead of taking the summer off after my regular school year job ended—being with my children and taking care of myself—I took on a summer position teaching workplace and personal budgeting skills to disadvantaged youth.

Between my jobs and graduate school, the workload was daunting. During those years I estimated that my time away from my family much of the year amounted to close to eighty hours a week, between work, college, therapy, internships, and the travel time for all that. I was so overwhelmed that although my family was also suffering, I couldn't see it. From the beginning, the process of therapy was made more stressful by the crazy schedule I was keeping.

That's when the depression took hold.

**************************1998-2003************************

Medication

Over a period of five years I was on no less than seven different kinds of antidepressants. My family doctor prescribed my first medication to alleviate the sadness, but when they didn't work,

Rion referred me to a psychiatrist (a medical doctor) for his expertise in medications for the brain. Several medications would seem to lift my depression, but made it hard for me to sleep. I'd feel better, but was always tired, so I would stop the drugs. I felt much more awake, but would slide back into depression. Another caused such brain fog it was hard to work. Some caused the sexual side effects of not being able to climax after arousal—just another nail in our marital coffin.

Using prescribed medication can be a good temporary stopgap. I've talked to other individuals about antidepressants over the years and each has a unique experience with what worked best for them. I'm not sure any antidepressant makes you feel completely normal, but they do help to varying degrees. They helped me handle the hard work of therapy once I found the right one for me. At any rate, no matter which drug I tried, I would often stop the drug because of its side effects and slide back into depression.

Stress

My antidepressant journey was a stress in itself and created more discord between my husband and me. I was leading an incredibly chaotic life, and because of this I started having anxiety and panic attacks with sweating and chest pains that made me think I was having a heart attack. The first time this happened, it facilitated more irritation from my husband.

"You're not having a heart attack," he stated.

It was late, the kids were asleep and I was struggling with chest pains and clamminess. My husband was in a conundrum trying to manage all of this. I was in a panic.

"I know but what if it is my heart? My chest has been hurting for hours."

I actually felt like I was about to die, even while intellectually I was telling myself that didn't make sense.

"I have to get help. I have to go. Call Mom. She'll come watch the kids or she can take me to the hospital."

So he called my Mom, and then, we ended up in the emergency room.

In the emergency department they performed all the tests to rule out physical causes of my chest pains and sweating. I finally was able to calm down enough for my more reasonable thoughts to integrate with my feelings that I was dying. I wasn't dying, I was having an anxiety attack. I felt foolish.

So while I was dealing with therapy for PTSD, and trying to restructure my memories to be stored appropriately, it was complicated by all sorts of other issues—medication, anxiety, my husband's career change, etc.—that also took time to manage.

My trip to the hospital occurred in January of 1999. I was given additional medication for anxiety and I bought a workbook on managing stress. It had a chart of stressors with a numerical rating of the amount of stress each item could create, including people, work, home, and money challenges, among other things. The number of stressors in my life was off the charts. Outside stressors made my life even more complicated and chaotic than my internal trauma was already making it.

The outside stuff was entering the therapy sessions, and the ensuing crisis took up therapy time. We were spending valuable hours discussing my anxiety over my husband and his career when we could have been working toward healing my PTSD. In a counseling class we were told that anyone in therapy for PTSD should reduce as many stressors and responsibilities of their lives as possible while they are working to heal. I wonder if I had reduced the responsibilities I was carrying, if I would not have been in therapy nearly as long.

We all have difficulties that color our perception of our own lives and the world around us. I didn't realize for a long time how much this stuff can make the work in therapy more taxing. Eventually I relied on supportive people who helped me identify and remediate some of these detractors. While eliminating everyone that made life difficult wasn't possible, I found that limiting exposure to stressful situations with difficult people was doable, especially those who did not depend on me or were not in my inner circle. I tried to sidestep people who required a lot of energy to deal with.

******************1999-2000*******************

Work

By six months into the therapy process, I had alleviated some of my anxiety. I still, however, had not learned to avoid taking on projects or making big life changes in the middle of therapy. In the Spring of 2000 I was about to take on summer work again for a second summer. I mentioned this with a sigh to Rion as I was headed out the door.

He responded to my tone of distress:

> "I can write you a statement for a temporary disability if you need it."
>
> "Thank you, but I don't need that. I should do this job for the money."

Suddenly it hit me how unreasonable my own expectations of myself were. My therapist had just told me I was in a state that he would call disabled, and I was actively choosing to do something that would make it worse. After seeing myself in this new light, I told my husband and the hiring agency that I was not going to take the summer job again. I felt like I had—finally—put my wellbeing first.

Eventually, through my own experience and in my counseling courses, I learned that I had to change to heal. Anything that didn't support the changes required throughout therapy could work against healing.

Support

I talked to God a lot. I plugged into music, which provided a good escape. I started talking to a few close friends and loved ones, especially my two sisters, and I spent time in nature. Choosing those healing activities over stressful obligations gave me a chance to think, to consolidate new perspectives with my own skewed ideas.

By early 2000, I was gaining perspective into myself and I was learning a lot. I talked to those who knew me best in a more open way than I ever had. I spent a lot of time in conversation with my sister and then wrote about it in my journal.

> *Talking to my sister was a gift today. She made me feel special. I can talk to her freely. I can be honest and work things out. Why do I resist that?*
>
> *She said something strange that Mom said about me. Mom told her I was always hard, because I had walls up and no one was welcome to intrude inside. Mom said she would have to wait until I was ready. My sister said the same thing; there are some areas where I will just cut off the conversation and she said she's afraid to go there because I will either get mad or cut*

her off completely. I said I know I do that, but I really need to be prodded. I can't talk about myself sometimes when I need to. But I want people to ask. My oldest best friend said that too. About my turning the conversation away, even though I really needed her to ask.

My sister did not quite agree that was all there was to it, though. She said sometimes there are lines you cannot cross with me. I let it go then, except I kind of understood. I was thinking about one of the times when Rion asked about our finances and I just cut that off, it was too much to get into, too intrusive. It didn't happen all of the time, but there were times I'd rather deal with things myself than have to explain anything.

So that's what woke me up at 3 a.m. thinking about these walls. Not the walls I want people to penetrate, but the solid ones. And how is anyone supposed to know the difference? And here I was blaming them, and still it comes back to me.

There is so much information that I have to think about and process before I can chance putting it out there for anyone else. Why? Because I need to have a presentation. I need to control what I put out there and how it's presented.

Wow, I don't let others take all the information in themselves and make their own conclusions. I know I worry that I won't be able to give out all the information because it's so disorganized that people will misunderstand, or maybe that I won't be able to buffer the truth, either for others or for myself.

But if I don't start I can't sort it out.

Therapist Notes November '98

11/6   Linda   **Individual Session**

Talking most of session about balancing roles of career and family. However, later said she had these discussions regularly and was not covering any new ground or feelings.

Interpreted as need to distance from feelings of last few sessions. Second time through story of her rape harder than the first. Closer to raw feelings. Very uncomfortable for her.

Reiterated that sessions move at her own pace. If she needs to slow down or back off it's her decision and OK.

11/10   Linda   **Individual Session**

Said she felt assaulted when being asked questions about the rape. Processed feelings. Processed her feelings about lack of power and discussed how to handle the situation and her feelings in the future.

11/17   Linda   **Individual Session**

Difficulty talking about feelings because it is "immodest" to bring attention to self.

Looked for ways to move beyond/past this.

Talked about PTSD diagnosis during sex with husband. Talked about the need for better communication and modification of behaviors to keep her grounded in the here and now.

Diagnosis: PTSD with Depression

Plan: Same   CBT (Cognitive Behavior Therapy)   RBK

CHAPTER 15

Depression

I had a history with depression. In college my angry and somewhat abusive boyfriend left me depressed with stress-related stomach and chest pains. A year later, after leaving that relationship, I had that humiliating sexual encounter on a date. I told myself I would never think about that again, but of course I did think about it. Depression came and went while I was in college. I might eventually have to talk about it.

In 1981, four years after graduating and six months after I was raped by the man who broke into my apartment, I met my husband, who also carried pain from traumatic experiences. He didn't hurt me as some others had, but while we loved each other and had good times, our relationship was often tumultuous and painful. As I write this, it occurs to me that in my young life I was drawn to injured souls. Or perhaps they were drawn to me and I was glad for the attention. At any rate, my husband once said that we go through life dragging the baggage of our lives behind us, and then we meet our life partner and dump our garbage over the other one's head—the metaphor for our marriage.

Life marched on as it always does, and over the years, we had plenty of fun as a young family loving our three boys. But then sometimes sad, shocking, or tragic things happen. That's life. In my life several things happened within a few years of each other. In 1992 my brother, who was a light in my life, died of AIDS. It was a heartbreaking loss. I started a full-time job in 1994 that took me away from my children. Then in November of 1995, within the period of a month, my youngest son, at six, was hospitalized with severe pneumonia. It was frightening. At exactly the same time my best friend called and said that her husband, also a dear friend, had just died of a heart attack and she needed me. Then my elderly and ill in-laws arrived for a long Christmas holiday and their dementia issues became obvious. The stress could not have been higher. That was when depression and anxiety began in earnest.

My husband blamed me for a lot of our difficulties. I knew that in addition to his career troubles, he had an unhappy relationship with his own mother. He transferred feelings about her to me whenever he would get stressed. He also (rightly) blamed me for not communicating my feelings to him. At the time, I didn't know what he was talking about.

Although those stressful years leading up to my PTSD diagnosis had me periodically depressed, it wasn't terribly intense. I was actually feeling pretty good that summer of 1998 when I started my graduate program, until I got hit with the flood of memories and flashbacks. Before long, getting into the quicksand of memories in therapy, the depression was back, but with all that I was dealing with, it wasn't entirely related to the rape.

Starting therapy and finally talking a bit gave me some relief, but I was obviously struggling. The sessions generally followed the same pattern, a little small talk at the beginning and then long silences waiting for me to pick what I wanted (or needed) to talk about.

But talk I must, and I had to start the conversation. So I began talking about my husband instead of about me.

> "My husband has been struggling. You know that his company lied to him about his compensation package. He's really stressed about money and he gets mad easily."
>
> Rion followed my lead. "So there's pretty constant stress between you and your husband?"
>
> "Yes. I don't know exactly how we're going to deal with this because you know, we have a lot of expenses with our house."
>
> *Don't talk about money! Leave this alone. Talk about good stuff.*
>
> "Anyway, my boys are doing well. My oldest is involved in everything, he's a good student and into band and sports. Our middle guy is incredibly talented in art and music. I keep thinking he'll be the Stephen Spielberg of the family. And our youngest is such a sweetheart, everyone loves him. He has his teachers wrapped around his little finger. All the guys have great friends."
>
> "You must be proud. How do your sons handle the stress between you and your husband?"
>
> "Well, we give them a lot of attention, and we have a lot of fun times together."

This was the pattern. I would maybe touch on issues we were facing and then wrap it up in a nice bow.

> "You have a lot of good things going on in your life. I can see that, but that's not what brought you in here. Can you talk about some of the things that are causing you problems?" Rion challenged.

Every time we met, it seemed to be the same. I would talk about my work, my counseling program, my previous position as a director at the Red Cross, my big, supportive family. I wanted to paint a picture of a healthy, together, accomplished life. I danced around problems.

Then I would touch on something.

"My husband gets mad at me about sex. It seems like he wants it all the time. He says I am his wife, and it is my duty to satisfy his needs. So I feel like I have to perform, to make him happy, and that doesn't feel good."

"Do you refuse? You have the right to make decisions about your own body."

"Well, sometimes, and sometimes it just feels contentious. That's when he tells me it's my duty. So I just go along."

"So you are not honest with him?" he asked pointedly.

"Um, I guess not. It seems like that would be a hard thing to do, so I just go along."

"Can you be honest?"

"I don't know. This is a really hard thing between us. I don't think being honest will go well."

Rion would challenge me to take responsibility for myself. I knew he was gently calling me out for being dishonest with my husband; the message wasn't lost that I blamed my husband for not reading my mind.

Eventually the discussion about my difficulty with sex led into talking about my experience in the rape. We had visited this topic many times over the first six months in therapy, but in February of 1999, Rion asked,

"Do you think your lack of desire is only about your busy life?"

I had thought about this before, but never too deeply because I didn't like to let myself think about the particulars of being raped.

> I responded, "I don't know. I am really busy and my husband has a much higher sex drive than I do. But I guess I do feel sometimes like I have to give in because if I don't, it will be bad."
>
> "Can you talk about that feeling; that it will be bad?"
>
> "I don't really like kissing. When that guy was on top of me, he was so gross. He was trying to kiss me, and I was just trying to keep talking so he wouldn't kiss me. I don't like it."
>
> I stalled so Rion asked, "What were you thinking about, at that time?"
>
> "Oh my God. It was so gross. I kept thinking, *Just talk about stuff. Don't think about what's happening. Keep him talking so he won't kiss me.* I also wanted to make him like me. I knew that when he was done, he might get scared and try to get rid of me."

My voice was getting smaller.

> "He was getting close to... being done. I started wondering if there was anything I could do to protect myself if he was going to try to kill me. There was nothing I could do. He was big and there was nothing I could use as a weapon. I remember wondering if I could use the bed sheet to protect myself. Of course, I couldn't. I realized I might be dying very soon."

In that moment, recounting it for Rion, I was immersed in how it felt to be staring at death, contemplating my murder.

> "I'm thinking about dying. Will it hurt? How long will it take? Everything is so big. It's all so big. Everything is in that one moment. It's so big."

I was small and frail. My voice was small and frail and choked with uncried tears.

I always talked about the vulnerable memories, my hidden thoughts, while staring down to the right. My memories of going through the hard stuff in therapy all involve that one spot on the carpet. When I finally raised my eyes, Rion looked rather stricken.

> He spoke, "That was awful. I didn't understand before. I am so sorry."

This time when I opened up about my experience, I went to a place I wasn't even aware of. This time, when I was vulnerable, Rion responded in a way that was kind of precious. I left the session feeling a bit lighter. Fresh air flowed through me.

For years after a good therapy session I would feel fresh, clean air breezing through tiny holes in the torso of my body. I felt heard, validated, open. I knew that sensation was a result of my therapist having broken little holes through the wall that I had built up, just little bits at a time, letting new air in. It was a fascinating phenomenon. I imagined it must be how a prisoner who was in isolation in a stuffy old cell would feel if a little hole of outside air suddenly poked through. That's how it felt: clean, new, fresh.

This was the course of my therapy for years, picking away at information hidden in my mind, pulling it out in bits and pieces, much like an archeological dig. Pieces of the puzzle that was me were discovered out of order and over time. Sometimes, we'd go deeper and then in subsequent sessions have to retreat, so I could sit with new shocks for a while until I could normalize my feelings. Everytime I opened up and was vulnerable was hard and doing it once didn't mean I could do it again. It was like building a muscle, I had to keep at it to get stronger.

And then, everything would come back in the middle of the night. The memories that I had let out of the closet would cause me to be anxious, withdrawn, and startled. Then I relapsed into my most severe depression.

Therapist Notes: 1999

2/16   **Linda**   **Individual Session**

Discussing rape. Specifically at the point when she felt if he were to kill her he would be doing it at that moment. Terrified and terrible waiting for that moment.

Visibly shaken.

5/28

Not as good at stuffing emotions. More conflict with husband. Finally talked it out with him.

Had done assignment to write a letter to the perpetrator several months ago. Could not share it until today. Powerful. Full of emotion. Pain.

Processed feelings.

Discussed what to do with the letter as it represents the emotion of the experience.

Diagnosis: Same: PTSD with Depression

Plan: Same CBT   RBK

The Worst of It

Recently, I was discussing some of the factors that can play into depression on a local radio talk show. I started by recounting some of my experiences as a school counselor working with teens.

"Some kids start filling themselves with negative self-talk pretty early on," I explained. "As a school counselor, I worked with kids who dealt with depression because they were so hard on themselves."

"Is this something parents put on their kids with their high expectations?" the interviewer asked.

"Sometimes, but it's not necessarily a parent thing. It's often the smart and high-achieving kids who feel like they need to really perform well to deserve all the love and praise they're getting. It's a tough thing to monitor from a parent perspective."

I had learned a lot about depression when I was dealing with it myself. I also read academic papers about negative self-talk for my counseling program. Over time, it started to make sense.

"So in my situation," I continued, "if I were corrected about something, I would start to chastise myself if I thought I wasn't measuring up. I'm the firstborn girl and I'm a people pleaser, so I was adored by my parents and extended family. I was on a pedestal. The problem is, I had to work hard to be perfect when I was on that pedestal. Once I started doing that, it just continued and got worse. The difficulty with self-talk is that no one else knows the conversations I was having in my head. It's hard to intervene when a child is filling themselves with negative self-talk. That's what I was doing."

"Can adults guard against that with their children, somehow?" the host inquires. "I mean, you don't know what's in your child's head."

"I think you can somewhat guard against it. There is a concept that thought is mediated by language. The words that we fill our minds with influence what we think about. For instance, I was incredibly hard on myself. That was from negative self-talk. I think of it now as depression being the thing that convinces us that the negative stuff we tell ourselves is true. I think if parents see depression symptoms or hear their kids beating themselves up for not performing at their best, it's time to intervene. Giving advice isn't helpful. It will fall on deaf ears if you don't know what the problem is. Asking questions and listening is required to find out what kids are telling themselves. That will allow parents to offer their child a different perspective, but it's a challenge. My mother was great at that, but I still beat myself up."

***********************1999-2002**********************

Explanations are great, but my story of working through depression in therapy wasn't helped by understanding the why of it (just like Rion had said). The experience of talking, of bringing my thoughts out in the open to be really examined, was new for me. I revealed my fears and discovered how terrified and in danger I had actually felt. To have Rion respond with such care and concern felt good and I felt lighter after. I was almost surprised by the depth of the depression that followed it.

One week after that breakthrough session, I was in therapy again, silent. Rion waited. Finally I spoke,

> "I've been kind of depressed since last session."
>
> He sat up straighter and looked surprised. "What's going on?"
>
> "I don't know. I just can't stop thinking about it and I think, why is this depressing me? It wasn't that bad. I didn't get hurt... Things are getting worse with my husband. I'm only able to sleep for three or four hours at night and I'm so tired I sleep during the day and that makes him mad. I'm not around enough for the kids. He's doing a lot."

And so began what became Major Depressive Disorder. It was overwhelming, but I was able to hide it at work and college. That meant that when I was home or with my family my depression was horrible. This continued for several years, right up to the beginning of 2002. As I was resolving many of the PTSD issues I had with the break in and rape, my marriage was melting down, and my boys were struggling with the contentious relationship between their father and me. I was adept at hiding things, but it was evident to Rion that there was something major I had not dealt with. I was depressed and anxious. I often felt in a state of dissociation—it didn't feel like my world was real. Things were numb. Because of my severe depression, Rion, as well as my mother and sisters, had fears about my potential for suicide. Rion had me in therapy sessions twice a week.

One Saturday morning, in late 1999, I was more than a year into therapy. I was hiding under the covers in my bed when I called my sister, who came to my rescue. When she arrived and came up to my room I told her, "I feel like I'm in hell. Honestly, I can't imagine hell being any worse." I trembled in agony. "This is different from physical pain. I feel like I'm being sucked in from my insides, like I'm a black hole. It's awful, I just need it to stop. I need somebody to make it stop. No one here understands. The boys need me, but I can't go out there."

My husband was angry with my self-indulgence. As I writhed in this emotional pain, his anger was pushing me further into the hole. I would crumple, figuratively and sometimes literally, into or behind the bed, once under the clothes hanging in the closet, anywhere I could escape. I was beaten down.

So I put it on my sister. She was desperate to help with no idea how to do so.

"What can I do for you?" she inquired.

"I don't know. I feel so alone, kind of in a space all by myself. I don't want to be alone. I want the boys to be okay. It's the weekend! They should be having fun, but their dad is mad and they're kind of stuck in the middle. I just need to get some of this craziness out of my head. Thank you so much for coming, it helps to talk about it. It feels less awful when I can explain it."

She smiled at me. "I'll come when you need me. You know I love to talk to you."

When she said this, I started to feel the pain of my turmoil fade. Reaching out and telling someone how I was feeling really did help. And my sister was full of fun. She would take the boys (and sometimes me) out for an adventure anytime she could.

When I was alone again, I started writing in my journal.

October 1999

What is this wall I'm behind? It has a lot to do with not liking things about myself and trying to keep those things hidden. I'm protecting myself by pretending other people don't see what I can't face, like how I feel really unattractive because I'm overweight. I believe I used to be attractive when I was thin. I might still be, but maybe I'm not anymore. I don't want to know either way, especially by soliciting that information. It feels immodest to even talk about it.

Rion says I'm afraid of my feelings, I don't know if that's why I bottle everything up, but I do avoid certain feelings—fear, embarrassment, and, of course, shame.

He asked if I was ever emotional about what happened. I talked to my older brother about when he came to be with me after I was raped. My brother said I was very matter-of-fact, which kind of surprised him, but then he didn't know what to expect.

I was matter-of-fact from the time I realized what was happening. I remember the shock of realizing that something awful, something unbelievable, unacceptable, was happening to me and I just talked to myself about how I needed to think to get through it. It was mostly just a thinking experience from then on. I had to recount it to the detectives, to the lawyers. Very matter-of-fact. I wanted to talk about my feelings, but since I didn't know how, since it's so awkward for me to bring up, I finally just stuffed it because I had to. I've done that a lot with upsetting stuff because it feels too awkward to bring it up, that calling attention to myself. I can't do it.

Rion started thinking that maybe what I am experiencing now is the "invasion" feeling that most people experience right afterward. It's like I finally felt how awful it was, like I only now picked up on the moment of realization that such an awful thing was about to happen to me. I was so shocked that I was being raped that I shut down for eighteen years. And here, the shock and everything, just seems to pick up from that very moment when I shut down before. I feel like all the years in between just vanished.

It seems all my emotions were so strong that I couldn't handle them. I haven't had strong negative emotions that I can't control in a long time. Just anger and humiliation. Adrenaline pumps for everything. If I'm angry, I want to hit. If I am hurt, I want to sleep. If I am scared, I am immobilized. If I am enthusiastic, I actually vibrate with nerves. If I feel love, I'm overwhelmed to almost tears. It's too much. So I keep feelings at bay in front of people for the most part. I almost forgot how powerful my emotions can be. And it hurt too much—old boyfriends, the rape, my husband, my brother's death, worry about the kids, about me. I panic.

I don't do emotions well. I am always over the top. Nothing is in moderation. Even positive is over-the-top and then I feel humiliated and that's unbearable.

Anyway, I think now I'm reacting to the rape. I'm still devoid of emotion, and I'm scared by the lack of control.

Therapy was obviously not quick or easy. Over the four years of therapy, revisiting issues that I thought were resolved caused more secrets to bubble to the surface. I had left that trauma to simmer for so long that many more troubles fell into the brew. Sometimes it felt like we would go round and round and end up back on a topic a year later. And I felt like a failure in a lot of regards: losing weight that crept on with pregnancies, being a wife who could make my husband happy, being a mom who my sons would be proud of, living up to my perception of my parents' expectations, etc., etc.

May 2000

There is a long list of goals I haven't lived up to. Maybe it's why I don't like to talk about myself to people. If I reveal my goals, I reveal myself as a failure or not having tried. For someone who is so hung up on how others perceive me, that is too dangerous. That's what I protect myself from. I think people will see that I don't have the discipline and character to achieve. It's not the conscious image I have of myself, but deep underneath, it's how I see myself. I want to hide that so others don't see it.

I was hiding from myself. Rion and I would often sit in silence. I couldn't think of anything to say. Then I would come home and just want to sleep. Sometimes when I did talk and we really got into the hard stuff that I have never wanted to think about or face, I would come home and be in an even blacker place.

At my next appointment, I was trying to explain to Rion what was going on. The first words out of my mouth were,

"I think about not living."

I explained how I got hung up on things I had said or done that I was sure people were judging. It would send me into full blown anxiety. It was excruciating. Depression had given way to anxiety and panic attacks, a pretty lethal combination. The suicidal thoughts had gotten bad.

"I don't have a plan," I continued. "I need this agony to stop, but I know no matter how awful I feel, if I kill myself, if I'm dead, it would ruin my boys lives. They are everything. I can't do anything that would hurt them no matter how awful this is."

"I'm glad to hear you say that," Rion stated. "I know you love your boys so much you wouldn't do anything to hurt them. And you are right. You would hurt them in a way they may not recover from if you took your own life. I know you are strong enough to endure this to the other side. That's your job as their mother, to put their needs first. So you have to take care of yourself to take care of them."

I prayed to God and I railed at God for not helping me out of this horrible situation, but hiding behind a wall of depression isolated me from hearing God. There were messages along the way that I wasn't alone, someone would make a comment to me in answer to a prayer I had just spoken in my head. God works through others and I had a lot of people helping me. But at the time, I couldn't always see it.

When I was really depressed and sought help from somebody to make me feel better, I would feel nurtured. It reinforced my depression when people were worried and tried to be caring and nurturing. This was another conundrum. It seemed like sometimes the only way I would feel that warm, cared for feeling was when I was very depressed and reached out for help. I had to work to overcome that situation. As good as it felt to be nurtured, it was not worth the pain of depression. I deserved to be nurtured at my worst and my best. I didn't need depression, I needed to talk.

My therapist's job was to hold my feelings in safety while I explored them so I could be more aware of myself. Rion was good at this, but I was bringing out difficult, sad, and angry emotions, and I started to feel anxious. I had spent so many years burying my feelings that it was a shock to reveal difficult emotions and feel their full impact. I had to be brave enough to open myself up and be vulnerable to another person.

When I finally was able to feel emotions beyond just anxiety and shock, I was able to really move toward healing. But emotions were only part of the work.

There were many thoughts about my experience and blame I turned on myself that I had to work through as well. It wasn't enough just to feel again. I had to make sense of how I responded to all the difficult realities in my life and what I was going to do with it all going forward. I had become depressed after remembering parts of my assault; the depression didn't abate on its own, even as I was opening up and finding some healing.

I was trying hard, but sometimes I felt so bad I just wanted it all to stop. I didn't want to be in this anymore. I would visualize stabbing myself, finally ending all the pain. I think that sometimes people focus on suicide when they are really trying to get somebody, ANYBODY, to do something to help them. It's a desperation thought about a desperation move. My fantasies were that attempting suicide would get people's attention, then maybe someone would help me. But I also realized that I couldn't be saved from the outside. People were already helping me—but to truly heal, I was going to have to participate in saving myself. I was going to have to turn to someone who would listen and say, "I hurt so bad I want my world to end."

The light at the end of this tunnel would mean relief from the pain of depression, anxiety and the craziness of PTSD. Living life beyond the hard stuff was my goal. While it felt like my years in therapy were just revisiting and re-experiencing a lot of my issues, the truth was I was learning and resolving a lot. I was learning how to talk to other supportive people when I needed to, I was getting exercise. I was thoroughly cleaning out my overstuffed closet of crap I'd stuffed in my brain throughout my life.

I had even told Rion in bits and pieces during the year 2000 about the date from college that had so humiliated me. I finally was able to label it as a rape, although because I felt responsible, I still wasn't able to tell him the details of what happened. At least now he realized that my unresolved PTSD and the wall I was hiding behind were about that date rape. The end of this journey and the healing that followed were close at hand. The discovery of what that would look like awaited me.

Therapist Notes 2000

1/20   **Linda**   **Individual Session**

Coming to some realizations concerning marriage. Could only go so far with feelings then needed to stop.

Processing issues concerning a second rape. Very overwhelmed. Guilt. Humiliation. Could not talk. More work to do here.

6/5

Stressed and depressed.

Intrusive recollections especially when falling asleep. Discussed strategies to focus on positive images at those times.

Began to discuss feeling about date rape—shock, humiliation, physical pain. Trying to work through, but frequently overwhelmed by feeling at those times. Working to ground self in the here and now. Put distance between self and those feelings.

7/20

Got a school counselor job. Very happy.

Continued to process strategies for dealing with assault. Doing better at not hiding. Given an assignment to draw "the closet" she goes into and the feeling in there. Depression continues.

10/30

Recognized dark place she can't escape when thinking of the second rape is really the dark camper in which she was raped. Can see windows and curtains now.

Some of its power is diminished. Good to give it definition then can be dealt with.

Still looking overwhelmed when discussing it, but not as much or for as long.

Diagnosis: Same: PTSD with Depression

Plan: Same CBT (Cognitive Behavioral Therapy
RBK

CHAPTER 17

Dear Rion (6/2001)

Dear Rion,

Thank you for suggesting I write to you.

There are so many things to say I don't know where to start. I've spent a lot of time and energy and more frustration trying to do this right. I've been very reluctant to bring up certain things, because of my perception of what you or whoever I'm talking to seem to be thinking. I know I should not do that. I know it is not accurate or even fair, but it still has a strong influence on what I will say.

I always played a great 'good girl.' I know I try really hard to be perfect and I'm trying now to give that up. It is so silly, but I don't even know who I am, because obviously I'm not perfect. But for me that was an identity. It's embarrassing.

I do appreciate it when you list topics I might want to talk about. It not only helps me focus, it gives me permission. I know that needing permission to talk about something is another issue I need to work on. But I am really, really slow.

I know I need to talk about that second incident from college. I've started to think maybe that humiliating experience was actually rape. You're right, I started getting depressed then, just trying to sort through it in my mind. I felt stupid, ashamed and responsible.

I suppose being strongly affected by what happened, but to not remember most of it should tell me that it's something you and I should discuss. It's just going to be so hard to go there and I'm so scared of the aftermath. I dread coming home and really sinking into depression again. Especially because this time I played a part in it.

That says a lot I guess. Thank you for this

Sincerely,

L.

CHAPTER 18

Coming Out from Hiding

O nce on this journey of discovery, trying to find a way to heal, there was no going back. It was September of 2001 and I had been in therapy for three years. I had worked through the break-in and rape and my buried fear about ending up dead afterward. We were working through issues I was having in my marriage—they weren't resolved, but I wasn't hiding them anymore. Still, I would often find myself driving and having a flashback. I'd have to pull the car over and wait for it to play out.

Rion knew by then that there had been another rape that I refused to talk about In therapy sessions. I had been able to admit the date rape from college, but for more than a year I couldn't say much about it. There was a tall, corrugated metal wall in front of my mind's eye, with all the words, emotions, and memories I didn't want to face on the other side. I couldn't talk about anything with that wall there.

I was still suffering from PTSD and for quite a while Rion couldn't figure out what had been so awful that it was still holding me back. There would never be any healing as long as I was on one side of the wall and the stuff I didn't want to face was on the other side. I was always going to be hiding stuff until I dealt with the worst of it. I knew that, and so, the session after I wrote that letter, I began discussing *the incident* in detail.

There have been things in my life that were worse, but this was the most humiliating. It had been twenty-five years. I had never completely forgotten about it—I told myself, when I entered therapy, that I was never going to admit it. Rion didn't understand for more than a year and I think he suspected something had happened to me in my family during childhood, maybe something that I wasn't remembering. But the truth is, I remembered—and I was hiding.

This wasn't stuff I had forgotten and shoved in the closet. This memory so shamed and embarrassed me that I went into the closet with it and wouldn't come out. I should have been getting better in therapy, but its poison had been leaking into me and making me sick.

This is the story I never wanted to tell, but It was time to suck up my courage. I started by writing about it, so I would finally be able to say it. I wrote it in the third person because it gave me some separation that first time of putting it out there. I started to read it to Rion that way.

Writing on the Truth Side of the Wall

She was just twenty years old and in college. She met him while tending bar. He was quiet and attentive. She doesn't remember why she was attracted to him. He was in his late twenties and owned a store and service business—a point in his favor.

He said he had been a troubled, foster kid, lots of misfortune with more than one dangerously abusive step-father. Though quiet, shy, and sweet, she was still embarrassed about going out with him. He had no social graces and he looked like what he was, hard-raised.

I stopped reading, suddenly embarrassed.

"This is ridiculous, Rion. You know this isn't a story about some girl; this is about me."

Rion was nonplussed.

"You can tell this in whatever way works for you. If you need to put it in the third person, that's okay."

Maybe it was okay for Rion, but I felt stupid. I felt like I was pretending it hadn't happened to me when we both knew that wasn't true. I was done pretending it didn't happen. Being truthful was the only way it would stop haunting me. So, hard as it was, I started being honest about the person in this story: about me. I put it into first person and kept reading. This was the first time I owned the experience, the first time I had ever spoken about it, outside of a moment inside my mind before I shut it into the closet.

I was already recovering from that experience with my abusive college boyfriend. A doctor had put me on tranquilizers. I don't remember what the symptoms were, but chronic stomach problems and chest pains were part of it. I was fragile. I didn't feel desirable to any guy I might really want to date, so I dated this guy.

I wish I could remember how our relationship went, but it's very fuzzy. I know we did stuff together for several months, riding his motorcycle, going out to bars, meeting some of his family. I don't remember much. We fooled around some, but nothing serious. I didn't want things to go too far, to be involved that way. I did not have birth control and told him that. I was pretty sexually immature, but we would get caught up in touching because it felt good. I felt desired.

One weekend, we set out to go camping, or maybe it was just a drive in the country. My memory is foggy, but we were driving his truck camper and stopped to picnic in a meadow. At some point after entering the camper, secluded in the country as we were, clothes were shed. I told him no intercourse and he decided I meant no pregnancy. We were necking and massaging each other and as I lay on my stomach getting a backrub he suddenly held me down, then was in me, telling me it was okay. He said I wouldn't get pregnant. Anal intercourse won't get you pregnant.

I couldn't believe this was happening. I remember my small voice begging, "Please. Please, stop." I was completely stunned by it. He ignored me. It was bad for me, unbelievable, but I chastised myself for even being in that situation. I played my part. I was mortified.

Then suddenly I was alone, lying there immobilized, completely shut down. Finally I dressed and came outside where he was waiting. All I clearly remember is standing in the meadow outside of the camper, in shock, thinking, 'I'll never talk about this. I won't think about it again. Ever.'

I don't have all the details. As I said, I told myself I was never going to think about it again. I don't remember if this was a camping trip or just a day trip. Eventually, I was back at school and he was gone. I think that was it.

Time was suspended as I stopped reading and sat there, repulsed by what I had just revealed.

"Are you alright?" Rion asked after a bit. "How do you feel to finally say that out loud?"

"Humiliated."

"Can you talk about that feeling?"

"Well, just saying it creates a visualization that I don't want anyone to have." (I didn't say "you" to Rion, I said "anyone." I already needed to depersonalize this exchange.)

"I can't believe I just did that, talked about it, created the visualization about me."

"Having someone force themselves on you without your consent is awful. It's shocking. You're brave to talk about it, but that sexual practice is not uncommon. What is so embarrassing for you?"

"Oh my God, just being in that circumstance at all. Having put myself there, and then *that*."

"Can you use the actual words of what happened?"

"Saying that we had sex...that way." I'm silent.

"Anally?"

"Yes."

More silence. Finally, I spoke,

"I hate even the thought of it. Sometimes I feel like I'm being probed by aliens. I can't stand the feeling. My eyes squeeze shut and I can't open them. It happens often when I'm in the car. I have to pull over and wait it out."

I'm repeating myself, but I can't state strongly enough how much I've wanted to skip this story. This is not the terrifying rape that made me feel that my life was in danger and started my journey into PTSD. But this is an important part of my healing because without revealing this experience, I would never have come out from hiding. I think part of my life would be lived on one side of a wall with my feelings on the other side. If I lived apart from my deepest feelings, all of my conversations in therapy, or any intimate conversations, would end up sitting on the surface of my emotions. I would have to continue hiding my true self, refusing to be vulnerable, being afraid to be embarrassed. I think being afraid to be embarrassed seems like an incredibly trite reason to sacrifice your authenticity, to sacrifice your emotions, to hide. I didn't want to be hidden anymore.

*******************************2023***************************

On that radio interview I had done about depression, I talked about my own depression catalysts.

> "I still have problems trying to hide from things I'm embarrassed about. Through years of therapy, now I know that when I'm sad and depressed or my mood is just flat, it's because something has embarrassed me or made me ashamed that I would prefer to hide. When I let stuff fester, it goes from a sliver to a generalized infection, which for me is depression. I'm trying to live a better life now.

When I saw Rion this past year for one of my infrequent check ups, I think he was stunned when I told him I was writing about my years in therapy with him. I am, after all, the person who was so easily humiliated I wouldn't talk. Now I'm telling the world this story. Rion was concerned if I would be able to navigate the fallout of baring my soul, of talking about my humiliation. It gave me the opportunity to clarify my intentions.

> "Honestly, Rion, I've argued with myself about this. I don't want to tell this part of my story, but if my writing isn't authentic, there's no point. I need to suck it up and be straight with people and maybe especially with myself. I have to be vulnerable. How can I write a book about the benefits of therapy and leave out the hardest stuff? I want to share what I've learned, that we all have painful experiences and some of us hide rather than deal with the hurt. If I can start to talk about this humiliating stuff, it kind of feels like, 'What's left to hide?' I still feel partly at fault for what

happened, but I'm realizing that I'm human. Sometimes we humans get ourselves in bad situations. We all have stuff we need to deal with. I think being brave and facing it is better than the alternative."

After coming to terms (somewhat) with my own experience, I have thought a lot about women in relationships that include unwanted sex. I'm curious about how women associate with men they are attracted to and the extent of what is considered date rape. I wonder about blurred lines and unclear communication. Over my years as a counselor I had many conversations with teens regarding their fuzzy approach to the physical aspects of dating. We certainly don't prepare our children to have clear and specific conversations about sex. I don't think we help them understand the nuance in romantic relationships enough. Media romanticizes sex, even the kind that's coerced or based on lies. Starting from childhood, sex is joked about, but seldom really *talked* about because that feels too personal. Sex conversations might be crass or joking, but seldom vulnerable.

I'm curious: what is it about being vulnerable that makes us shy away from it? I now know that being truly vulnerable in a conversation, getting to the deeper stuff, feels good, but for such a long time it was my greatest fear. As I tried to understand what prevents vulnerability, I thought about it from a military perspective. Unguarded areas are open to attack. When we become vulnerable in sharing our innermost thoughts and feelings, that knowledge can be used against us. It's why the more we get hurt in our lives, the more we protect ourselves from it happening again.

I continued to explain my decision about including this chapter to Rion:

"I want every woman who has been in a sexual encounter that she did not expressly give permission for to feel vindicated. It took me a long time to become that brave, and I come from a healthy background. But I also believe we have to accept responsibility for fixing ourselves, which is another good reason for being in therapy. It's why I have to include my story about the date rape. My being brave enough to do this might inspire readers to be brave enough to tell their own story, and that will help them heal."

Our society has trained girls to be pleasers, to be the givers in relationships, to play the part of the weaker sex. This is so ingrained in the way our society operates that we often don't recognize the implicit messages of subservience. We've all heard the admonition about sex: "No means No." But what happens if you just don't say *Yes*, maybe don't say anything, or you try to deter certain activity and get talked into sexual play you didn't really want?

If we don't express clear and *enthusiastic* consent for someone to touch or enter our bodies, it should be off limits. Enthusiastic consent should be freely given, reversible, informed, and specific, meaning every type of sexual activity, every time with anyone, including our partners. I've had some occasions when I've turned my head away from an unwanted kiss or tried to move hands away that were touching me. I don't know why I didn't just say, 'stop that.'

What I have realized is that *why* it happened isn't important. It's how we feel about the encounter that matters. If I leave a sexual encounter that I didn't want or that went too far because someone used some form of power over me, be it mental, emotional, or physical, it affects me. Being upset and angry about something like that is okay. Being upset and chilling with it until I internally give the person who injured me the excuse of meaning no harm causes me to turn the pain inward. Sadness descends into depression when I turn anger on myself.

If it feels like rape, it is rape. Whether it's prosecutable or not, it left a scar that needs to be dealt with. I've felt responsible and have hidden it away in that closet for years. It affected me. It affected people in my life. I'm not alone in this.

Have I healed enough to feel this journey is almost over?

My experience of PTSD in my therapy was being resolved, but I still had issues and work to do before I no longer needed the help I was receiving.

L. FEIG KNIPE

THEME 3

THE PROMISE

L. FEIG KNIPE

CHAPTER 19

Letting Go

Will therapy improve my marriage?

My first husband was the baby of his family. Very early in our relationship, I discovered that he had a pained childhood with experiences that left emotional scars. He idolized his dad, a gregarious and involved older father who traveled for work and who died when my husband was barely out of his teens. He was reluctant to introduce me to his much younger mother, which I thought odd until I met her. Turns out, she was quite the character. She had different ideas about friendships, parenting, and men, whom she didn't trust.

For example, when our boys were little, we visited her for a week. During this visit, she told me about her own childhood:

> "We traveled across the country in a covered wagon. Mother died when I was very little," she started.
>
> "That must have been very hard for you. Who was traveling with you?"

I was fascinated that there were still covered wagons in the early 1900s and she had traveled that way.

> "My father and my older brothers. I have sisters who are a lot older. They got away as soon as they could. You know, we girls are expected to *take care* of the men."

Suddenly, by the cryptic way she offered this information, a lot of things made sense. She never admitted anything outright, but her simultaneous attraction and disdain for men, the way she belittled and ranted at my husband as a child, and what she said about men, made me think she may have endured abuse herself.

She had scars from the hard and motherless life she led as a little girl.

I resolved to never let my boys be alone with her.

This was far removed from my experience of a loving, supportive family, but the effects of our much different traumas were similar. My husband and I were like the walking wounded. There were a lot of control issues between us, typical of individuals in our situation. We dumped our garbage on each other.

We had different parenting approaches, and we argued often about it. I feared for my boys. Life was scary and I worried about everything. Meanwhile, his relationship with his mother was fraught and unhealed; when he became frustrated he would rant at me, spewing onto me a lifetime of anger toward his mother. It wasn't good for our marriage and it wasn't good for our boys to witness.

So while I was making improvements in my mental health, the journey was *not* almost over. We were entering the shadow of a marriage on self-destruct. We started to attend couple's therapy where my husband again detailed his complaints about me. As usual, I sat in stony silence. I wasn't good at couple's counseling, and I was more shut down than ever. I could talk to Rion now, but to a new therapist? And in front of my husband? I simply was not that brave.

> "She doesn't say anything when she talks. She hides a lot, I feel like I'm parenting alone. Everything is on my shoulders."

The therapist looked at me and asked what I had to say about his complaints.

Swirling in my head, heard by no one but me, was my defense:

He'll never see everything I do. I work hard at my job at school forty to fifty hours a week, I'm in college another fifteen, and then doing homework. Then add all the therapy I'm getting. There are hours and hours of travel time for it all. I can't stop any of this if things are going to improve. I take care of the boys and the house all the rest of the time.

I can't quit my job—I need a job, I need to make money. That's exactly what he wanted me to do. He's unhappy in his work, and he's not making the money we expected or needed on his own. He's depressed and I don't want to call attention to all that. I'm doing as much as I can to help with the income, with the family, with the house. But I know I'm distant. I know when we fight I hide, and then I'm removed even more. But that's all he sees, that I'm not around. He doesn't see why I'm not around.

But I couldn't explain all of that so I sat there in anger, feeling hopeless. I didn't say anything. I knew I'd sound like a bitch if I did. I didn't think I was to blame, but that would mean *he* was to blame, and I didn't want to hurt him by implying that.

So I didn't talk.

My husband continued,

> "I can't keep doing this. We should just call it quits and move on."

The therapist had been waiting months to hear this from one of us. He asked how I felt about that statement.

> "I'm done," was all I could say. In my mind I was relieved. I knew it was coming, but I don't think I had the courage to say it myself. I was grateful that my husband did.

Our therapist jumped into action and started to talk through the steps of what was next. It was overwhelming at that moment. We had been married for nearly twenty years and our entire outward focus was to fix our marriage and stay together. Even though I had been harboring thoughts of an imminent split, and although my husband told me he had always expected me to leave him, we couldn't believe it had just been decided.

We left in a daze.

In reflection, if I had talked and let the therapist do his job, we may have come to the understanding that we both contributed to our troubled situation, and maybe we could have found a different solution. I knew I had never been taught how to confront anger. My family had so many people in our house that in order to prevent World War III, anger had to be tamed. Treating each other with kindness was expected, voicing our aggravation with each other was not encouraged. Retreating to our rooms to calm down was the policy—at least that's how I interpreted expectations of handling conflict. I was good at retreating. But retreating clearly wasn't working with my husband.

The next time I saw Rion, I tried to explain what had been happening.

> "Well, after that couples counseling session where we talked about ending our marriage, my husband refused to talk about it at home. It had sounded pretty final, but he acted like nothing had really been agreed on. Finally, I insisted we

talk to the boys. We did, and it was awful—it was so sad. They were crying, then we were all crying.

"Afterward, I was upstairs and I felt like I wasn't in my body anymore. I kind of felt next to myself as I was walking down the hall. It was so strange. So uncomfortable."

"It is uncomfortable," Rion said, "but it's normal. You were feeling shock and sadness in the moment rather than compartmentalizing those feelings in your mental closet and just moving on. It's normal to feel the way you feel. You should be having uncomfortable feelings. This is a lousy situation in your life. It doesn't feel good, but you are *feeling* your emotions, and that is good."

Well shit. I don't like feeling this way—feeling instead of stuffing is uncomfortable. I don't like being uncomfortable.

But, I have to admit: it is progress.

Life is hard, but at least now I'm aware of myself and my circumstances. This is knowledge I'd been hiding from for a long time.

One of the things my husband and I got right was getting into therapy. That was the right choice for us. We didn't want the outcome that we got, however. We separated. We split up our family, even though we loved our family and loved each other. We never wanted that to happen, but as I have said, sometimes you have to give up something you love to get something better. This is what happened for us. It was hard, of course, but after the separation we both became happier. As a co-parenting, divorced couple, we were much healthier and loving toward our sons and to each other.

After we separated the turmoil stopped for us, but our sons were suffering from a broken family. The first year after we split was tough. We sold our big house in the country, and my ex got a little apartment in a community twenty miles away. The boys and I moved into a much older and more affordable house that I bought. My oldest was grateful to be headed to college. The rest of us, Mom, Dad, and boys, still went out sometimes as a family and had a good time, but it felt strange. On one of those occasions at a festival, I laughingly said to their dad, "I'll date you, but I'm never going to live with you again!" It was a joke, but it was true, and we both knew it.

We hadn't finalized the divorce, but it was coming. Throughout the process of separation, I kept asking myself one question: *Will I be a better mother after all this?*

In the mid 1990s, several years before my descent into the hell of PTSD, my sister and I were having coffee while our youngest kids played.

> "You know," I said, "I have this feeling that things in my life are so good that at some point the other shoe is going to drop"

> My sister looked at me strangely.

> "What do you mean?"
> "Well, things are great: I have wonderful kids and a good marriage and the house we dreamed about, but for some reason I just feel like it could all go away. I feel like something bad will happen."
> "I don't see the great life you're talking about." My sister has always been straightforward in her sentiments. "You have struggles in your marriage and money is an issue since you built your house. You have lots of other problems you talk about. It's great that you see the positive, but I don't think you have to worry about the other shoe dropping, because I don't think everything is as great as you think it is."

Funny that I remember this one conversation so clearly. It was a premonition.

Less than a decade after that conversation, my husband and I were separated and headed toward divorce—and on the other side of the 'other shoe dropping.' My PTSD symptoms had mostly resolved. After four years of therapy, I was learning how to be open with my feelings and how to talk about them. But as much as I had personally progressed, it was a hard time all around for the family. My oldest was about to leave for college. Their father had left and we were selling the house that we loved and built together in the country.

My college bound son and I were on a walk, talking about it all.

> "Mom, I always thought our family was normal. Going to stay at Gramma and Granddad's at the lake and all the travel we did, hanging out and doing fun things together, I thought we were happy. But when I talk to my friends now about their families, I can see maybe we were never as healthy or normal as I thought. I know we haven't been these last few years. I don't remember if we ever were. I'd like to think so, but I don't know."

Looking back on my conversation with my sister, it occurred to me that maybe we were all living in denial about the problems in our family. Children are not expected to be able to see what's normal and healthy. Adults should be able to do that. Hiding as I did kept me from looking at anything too deeply. Therapy required me to confront my reality.

> "You know, darling," I said, "how much fun it is with your aunts and uncles and cousins when we're all together—how great Gramma is to be around? That's how it was growing up for me and that's what I wanted to give you guys as your

mom. You are all amazing—you're wonderful, caring, and loving, and you deserve better than what we've been giving you. Your dad and I have been struggling with our own mental health for quite a while, but we were mismatched from the start. It doesn't mean we don't love each other, but we don't live together well. We don't approach life and interactions the same way. When your dad gets mad, he needs to be able to confront those issues and it gets scary for me. I shut down, and then he gets scared and becomes more condescending to try to make me talk. It hasn't been good for you guys to see that. I really regret that we haven't been an example of how to have a good relationship. I think we will all be healthier as we move forward with your dad and me living separately."

To love our children and build up their self-esteem and interpersonal skills was what they needed. Sometimes we were great at this, but for periods, when my husband and I were suffering from financial troubles and mental health issues, things were bad. Instead of building my children up, my fears caused me to try to control them. I worried about everything, the kind of trouble they could get into, how they treated us and each other. Whatever I thought was a good and healthy person was what I tried to force onto my sons. It isn't ever helpful to try to control anyone, it certainly wasn't for our kids.

Giving into our fears for the bad stuff that might happen caused us to try to control them, which sent the message to them that they were not good enough on their own—that they needed us to direct and punish to teach them in order for them to be good, or kind, or successful enough. That message of not being good enough can stay in one's head forever. I have learned in the many years since then that loving our children, setting a good example, and letting them know that we believe in their goodness allows them to grow into the people they are meant to be.

So my boys had struggles as they grew into their teens and beyond, navigating the journey without consistent parenting. Their dad and I tried to be good parents, but the understandable truth is they were often furious with us, so we were less helpful when they needed us. This persisted through their adolescence, well beyond our separation. But our situation improved through therapy and by removing the dysfunctional partnership we were in. Then we could work on being better parents and generally getting healthier.

I was getting healthier. There were so many breakthroughs in therapy that suddenly the floodgates opened. For all the years I never cried, now I cried every time I talked about anything emotional, whether it was good or bad—both inside therapy sessions and outside of them. I cried every time we drove past a house that looked like the one we built and had to sell. I cried a lot. We were a newly separated family but after years of listening to their father accuse me of being manipulative, they thought that my tears were an attempt to try to control them through emotional manipulation. It just made them mad. I was embarrassed about crying so much, but I couldn't control my tears.

So here's some learning: I can't control my kids, and I can't control myself. I can't control things.

***********************2024************************

Years have passed since then. My sons are now grown and all are husbands and fathers with loving, supportive wives and adorable children. My daughters-in-law are warm and loving. I'm lucky to have each of them in my life. I get to be involved with my sons' families in the ways they and their wives desire. My role is to be a good listener and respect their perspectives without judgment, something I regret not being better at when they were young. I respect their parenting decisions and the life decisions they are making for themselves.

I am in awe of the wonderful job this new generation of parents is doing. I'm glad my boys haven't followed our worst examples and pray they listen to their children in the tough times rather than try to control them. I hope perhaps they gleaned some good examples from us. I would like to believe that. As time goes on I see evidence of it, but I know the credit goes to them.

I used to say to Rion that I worried a lot about screwing up my kids.

> "You do the best you can raising your children," he replied.
> "It is their job to fix anything that isn't working for them when they grow up."

A more recent discovery for me: being a grandparent is easier.

CHAPTER 20

Relationships

Will my relationships be better after therapy?

What would it actually feel like to express anger appropriately or to feel joy again? Instead of little pinpricks of air moving through my body, how would it feel to have fresh air all the time? Could I bring a pure, clean, healthy feeling to my relationships, instead of being guarded at every interaction?

Time went by and eventually I stuck my toe into online dating. The boys' dad did the same. I dated a bit while he met a wonderful, successful woman whom he loves and respects. She told me that he was the love of her life and that made me happy for them. Theirs is the relationship he was always looking for. It wasn't with me, because that isn't the kind of love we had. I'm glad he finally found it with her.

Only my youngest son was still living at home, and he would be with his father most weekends. He adored his step-mom. We spent holidays together, the boys, their dad, his wife, and me. My oldest and middle son both began relationships with wonderful girls, who became part of the fabric of our growing, blended family.

I continued to date, but I was tired of the dating game, realizing I didn't even know what was fun for me anymore. For twenty years in my marriage, all my fun was wrapped up in kids and family. Dates would ask what I liked to do for fun, but I didn't know.

Eventually, I canceled my online dating membership. Two days before my subscription to the online service was to expire, I took one last look—and saw a delightfully quirky and accomplished guy named Bob. His pictures made me laugh out loud and his profile sentiments sounded like he had written expressly to me. I messaged, "I just stopped my search. You are the guy I was looking for."

Bob told me that message was so bold he was taken aback. But he read my profile and we had so much in common that he immediately replied. We met a few days later, and he was as delightful as he seemed. I was right—he was the one I was looking for. Over the next few months, I started to realize that his profile had barely scratched the surface of the brilliant and wonderful man he was. We dated and within months fell in love.

I met the love of my life. After years of therapy, thank God, I was ready for him.

I was still seeing Rion for appointments but much less frequently. A lot of the time in our sessions we would just discuss my going forward in life as a single, dating woman. I was afraid I'd just continue being a people-pleaser, but it turns out that everything I had learned in our work together had made me a more confident, bold, and open person.

"I met someone who is really special. I'm nervous because I'm afraid it might not last, but he always tells me when I'm leaving his house to drive carefully because he wants me in his life for a long time. I love it when he says that."

"He sounds like a special person," Rion responded. "What is his name? What does he do?"

"Bob. He's a college Dean. He's involved in a lot of community organizations and musical stuff…on the go all the time. It seems like everyone knows and likes him."

"What do your boys think of him?" Rion inquired.

"They're always standoffish about anyone I date. They'll say I'm settling or something negative. But they like him; they think Bob is okay. He knows how to talk with them. He also has two really nice sons, a daughter-in-law, and a granddaughter."

"That sounds good."

"It is good. And he's easy for me to talk to. We talk about everything. He doesn't want to get married again, though. At least that's what he said online. That makes me cautious."

"Caution is good." Rion encouraged. "It will allow you to take things slowly and really decide if this is a good relationship for you."

"I know. It's just really hard, not knowing. It's all out of my control, I know that."

"Yes it is. But now you do know that, and it even seems sometimes like you're getting more comfortable with the lack of control."

In another meeting with Rion I told him about a dream.

"I had a dream that Bob and I were in his truck and he got out, but I was sitting in the passenger side when this huge bear started to climb up on the hood of the truck and was breaking through the windshield to get at me. I was just frozen with fear. The bear almost got me when Bob threw open the passenger door and pulled me out into his arms and carried me away. He saved me. I've never had that feeling before—someone taking care of me like that."

From then on, and throughout those final months of my PTSD, Rion used my feeling of Bob as my savior as a healing tool. If I felt like I was dissociating or I was anxious, he suggested I think of Bob taking my arm and pulling me out of the upsetting situation. With time, using that visualization, I no longer had any anxieties. I no longer dissociated.

My relationship with Bob continued to deepen. We talked about what we wanted in our lives, both as individuals and as a couple. I became more comfortable with not knowing everything, and all the while, I was being completely honest about what I wanted in a relationship. I didn't give ultimatums. I left it in Bob's hands to decide what he wanted as well.

When I finally decided I needed to know where I stood, we were almost a year into dating. It was a warm night in late spring and we had been cooking and had dinner on his patio, the most relaxing place for us to spend time together. Eventually, as we chatted and relaxed into the conversation about our summer plans, I became brave enough to step into the delicate topic of marriage. Still, I was in my own head trying to word my question in a way that wouldn't disrespect Bob's assertion that he wanted to remain single. I got up to give myself some time to gather my courage, and I started to clear the table. I headed to the kitchen and Bob followed. As I set dishes on the counter, without looking at him, I said,

> "So…you said you don't want to get married, but do you want to live together?"
> "Why yes, I would like to live together!" he replied enthusiastically.

My heart leaped in my chest! I had expected this response but at the same time I doubted that I would ever be so lucky. It didn't change my resolve, however, to be honest about my feelings. I looked up and turned to face him.

"I would too, but I'm not going to live with anyone without being married. I just can't set that example for my boys."

"Actually, I don't think I would be comfortable with it either," he agreed.

I continued pressing the discussion.

"Will you make me a promise? It's really important to me that if you realize this is not going to be a permanent relationship that you tell me when you realize that. Would you promise to do that, please?"

"I promise to be honest with you," he conceded.

"I am protecting my heart. As long as you're unsure about us having a future together, I can't fully let myself fall in love."

This all concerned Bob greatly. He said he never thought so much about a relationship in his life as that first year we dated and had those discussions. He also said he had never before talked about the things we talked about. I was open with him, and he was with me. It was new relationship territory for both of us.

During the week, when my youngest son, a high school junior, was with his father, I would often go to Bob's after work to have dinner with him. It was another kitchen counter moment a week after Bob's and my discussion about living together. My mother called on my cell phone.

"Hi Mom!" I answered.

"Oh! You're with Bob!" was all she said.

"Yes, but how did you know?"

"I can hear it in your voice. You're happy when you're with Bob."

I was still taking antidepressants and it was a struggle, even though I was so happy in Bob's presence. I had already told him about my depression just months after we started dating. It was a revealing admission. We had been sitting on the sofa talking about our medications, the kind of personal sharing older people do. Bob said he took a pill for his high blood pressure and I admitted I took antidepressants. He didn't quite know how to take that information. To my surprise, he said he'd never been in a relationship with someone with depression and was curious if I still struggled even while on medication. I told him that yes, sometimes I did, but it helped most when I could talk about it. At my next therapy appointment a few weeks later, I brought him with me to meet Rion. During that session, Rion helped Bob understand what to do if I seemed depressed. If he helped me talk, I would be better.

We had lots of discussions over our first year together about letting life play out without trying to control it. On the first anniversary of our meeting, Bob gave me an anniversary card. It was long and carefully worded and I was touched. I showed that card to my mother, sisters, and friends over the next few weeks.

The message in the card read:

> *My Dearest Linda,*
>
> *I am so happy you're in my life. Daily I remind myself how lucky I am. You complement me, you complete me, you make me happy. Thank you!*
>
> *The worst that can be said is that we are both smart, caring, talented, hardworking, funny, competent, and interesting people... separately.*

Together, we're even better. Scary though it is when I allow myself to think about it (pinch me! pinch me!)—I do enjoy the exploration.

So... as a permanent team, think what we could do... and enjoy doing it, growing together? There'd be no stopping us.

What say we start working on the details of how that dream can happen?

I'm in if you are.

I love you,
Bob

Everyone I showed Bob's message to said how happy they were for me. But then they would each ask,

"But what does he mean?"
"I don't know!" I replied.

It was several weeks after the anniversary of our first date and the message in the card. We were going to be traveling to see his mother in a few days and I needed to be clear about his intentions and what exactly we would be telling her and everyone else. We had gone to dinner at a restaurant near the water and afterward went out on a dock to watch the sunset. I couldn't delay any longer and I asked him what exactly we were going to tell his mother. He said,

"We'll tell her we are going to have a ceremony to celebrate our love and commitment to each other."
"What kind of ceremony?" I pressed.
"A commitment ceremony," he replied.
"I don't think I'm quite clear on what you mean. What is the commitment ceremony you have in mind? I need to know for myself too."

This back-and-forth exchange went on for a while in a frustratingly funny way. Bob was not trying to be funny, and I could tell that he wanted to ask me to marry him but he couldn't say the word. I had been very respectful about Bob's reticence to discuss marriage for the past year, however, I didn't realize until this moment that he struggled to actually say the word. I tried to help.

"Bob, I want you to know that it would be an honor to go through life as your—"
"Stop!...I can do this!"

He paused for a long moment. I wanted to help but he shushed me again.

Finally he blurted, "Will you m-m-m-marry me?"

I was so shocked he actually said it. I laughed with joy, but as I was answering him, my eyes clouded and my voice became husky with emotion. I reached over and put my hand in his.

"Yes! Absolutely! I'd be honored to be your wife."

We got married two years to the day after we met. We had a funny story to tell and from that day forward he would say to me,

"I love you. Will you marry me?"
My reply: "In a heartbeat."

We became a big, blended family, all of us parents, spouses, former spouses and children. We were friends, all of us.

I still struggled with depression sometimes, but Bob would see the real me because he paid attention, and because I had the courage to show him. He would help me practice talking in the safety of his care until I understood what was bothering me. I started to become more vulnerable and it deepened our relationship. In return, he would have a practical, non-judgemental perspective that helped me accept my feelings and my situation. My depressions became much less frequent in my sixteen years with Bob, to the point where they were almost non-existent. That was our relationship.

Over time, I learned that my openness benefitted not just me and my close relationships but others too. As I learned to be genuine with people, to show myself with all my faults and vulnerabilities, people began to tell me things they'd never said out loud before. I can now bring up confidences I used to keep hidden, and people feel safe doing the same. When I just need to talk, I am discerning about who I am safe opening up to. Likewise, even with difficult people, I try to be caring and thoughtful for those who need understanding. I know how it feels to need consideration. I owe it to others to be thoughtful, because there was a time when I was that difficult person. This was a time of growth and openness, and I was so glad to be with Bob throughout it.

All relationships eventually come to an end, however. We don't dwell on that inevitability, we don't even like to acknowledge it, but it's life. I loved Bob with all my heart, and he died. Afterward, I missed him so much that sometimes I couldn't breathe. We were both surrounded by people who cared for us, family, friends, and colleagues. And then they cared for me afterward.

I waited for the depression to come back. I expected it. I was ready for it. But it didn't come. Instead, I just felt grateful. I knew our marriage would not be forever, not in this world, and I miss him, but I was ready for Bob. Bob's legacy for me is gratitude and joy, I was grateful that I had taken that long, hard journey braving therapy because when the most magnificent person I ever met came into my life, I was ready when he chose me.

CHAPTER 21

Healthy Life

When I was a school counselor, I worked with students who had to deal with mental health and other issues that complicated their attempts to heal, much the same as my experience. There are many ways to deal with complex emotional pain. Some drown the discomfort with food, alcohol, or drugs. Others hurt themselves to overwrite the mental anguish with physical pain. Gambling, shopping, and other ways to go through money can also be addictive behaviors used to self-medicate, but all this complicates healing. Personally, I gained quite a bit of weight in my years of crisis because I used food to escape. I also would eat up hours online or shopping. Once you pick your poison it's hard not to revert to it when you want to escape. I try not to let myself avoid issues anymore, and I also try not to rely on food. I'm on guard against those tendencies, but it's always a work in progress.

This chapter is about how I've built a healthier life through good habits and planning to maintain the benefits of therapy.

******************2002*****************

Everything felt disorganized, my thinking and my life. I was sitting in Rion's office, but in my mind's eye, I literally saw filing cabinets along the wall with papers from the file drawers scattered everywhere on the floor, at least six inches deep. They contained all the issues and stories of my life and were completely out of order. I didn't know where to start with this mess.

"There are papers all over the floor," I said.
"Just pick up any paper and tell me what's on it," Rion would say.

It took a long time, but when I was able to do that and as we talked through the items, we were able, finally, to put them in order. The chaos in my mind was finally getting filed where it belonged.

After years of hard work, I reached a point in therapy where I no longer suffered from all of the symptoms of PTSD, and the confusion of my life.

*******************The Present***********************

Now to stay healthy, I have to keep both my environment and my life organized. This is a helpful strategy for more than just physical surroundings. When my environment starts to get messy, my thinking gets messy, my activity declines, and my eating gets worse. So it's important for me to keep my surroundings organized, with everything where it belongs.

Healthy living and a life free of messes requires ongoing maintenance. My goal is to be energetic, clear-minded, ambitious, motivated, and future-oriented. I want to be mindful of the moment I'm in and to live a productive and purposeful life. My desire is to be happy with an appreciation for life and a sense of wonder. I want joy.

To achieve my goals, if I focus on my physical, mental, social, and spiritual health, my experience is that I will be motivated to exercise, maintain a healthy diet, have healthy internal dialogues, and be in charge of my time.

Planning is key.

Diet

Food has always been my nemesis, so I will start with that.

I am a member of Weight Watchers, having lost my excess weight through the program and the group support of their meetings. I continue to attend on a regular basis as a Lifetime Member in order to keep the weight off. I was recently at a meeting, sharing with the group:

> "For years, I would wake up and lie in bed thinking, '*Today is the day I'm going to start eating only healthy food. I'm going to start my diet today*.' And then, every day by halfway through the day, the temptations of whatever food or situation I was confronted with would dash my plans. The very next morning, I'd lie in bed, berating myself, and saying, 'Today is the day I'll start my diet.'"

Weight Watcher members nodded their understanding. I was not alone. I choked up as I finished my thought.

> "When I started Weight Watchers six years ago, my self-criticism stopped. I manage my eating now. And I come here for your support to stick with it."

Being heavy was something that always bothered me, even though most of the time I wasn't terribly overweight. After college, I moved to Florida and spent a lot of time at the beach, so I joined Weight Watchers for the first time and lost thirty pounds. I felt more attractive, confident, and healthier. I maintained my goal weight for a dozen years (into my marriage and first two pregnancies) by remaining physically active and keeping a mindset about what I should be putting into my body. I also continued with the social support by attending the meetings. When I was pregnant, I would gain significant weight and then lose it on the program after my boys were born … until my third son. I started to lose the pregnancy weight, but I also started working again when he was just two months old. By the time my little guy was nine, I was into full-blown PTSD. Life got away from me.

My descent into obesity after my PTSD began is very similar to my journey into mental illness and all of the co-occurring issues that fed into it. I didn't keep up physical activity or the support of the group. Things got more crowded in my life between family, work, college, and therapy. My mindset became scattered. We ate out at fast food restaurants frequently, and I gained more and more weight—many more pounds than I had initially lost upon moving to Florida twenty years before.

I'm now a Weight Watcher living in a healthy body again these past six years and I will continue with the support. I try to regularly revisit my diet to keep to my weight-management journey. I make healthy food easily accessible, so that is what I reach for. I drink a lot of water, because I often interpret thirst as just a need to put something in my mouth (like food). When I am in control of my eating, I don't tend to beat myself up. It's important for my mental health as well as my physical health.

Exercise

A top priority was to get stronger and more fit and then keep at it. If I don't, especially as I age, I'll lose muscle very quickly. I learned that exercise helps our mental health by the physical good it does for our bodies. It helps our brains and bodies clear out toxins, get stronger, and feel better. It's good for our well-being.

I am now a healthy weight and get regular exercise. At a recent WW meeting, we had a discussion on how to incorporate exercise into our week. One of the members shared, "I realized what was keeping me from exercise was that I was always thinking about doing it at an inconvenient time. So I found three times a week where I could conveniently exercise and I put that in my calendar and I stick to it."

Our coach stated, "A lot of exercise options I'd tried in the past were things other people were excited about, but did not motivate me. So, I kept looking for activities I thought were fun. Once I found activities I loved, I became a regular exerciser because I look forward to it."

This was a typical discussion at a meeting. It is the value of community, because other members' ideas helped me find new ways (or remind me of things that helped me in the past) to be true to my own commitment—something I struggle with, especially during our dark and dismal Northeast winters, when it's harder to go outside.

When I was first losing the weight that I had gained over the past nearly thirty years, I was newly retired. I was feeling better as the pounds came off, but I was weak. My difficulty was I didn't particularly like to exercise, at first because I wasn't strong so it was hard, and later because I would just get busy with other things. It seemed an inconvenience.

Then my middle son told me they were expecting a baby. I realized that if I was going to be in good shape for my grandchildren, I needed to get stronger. I started to go to the gym. I used the weight machines or free weights and the bike. I gained muscle and it got easier. Then it started to feel good. Whenever

I exercise, I feel better, stronger, energized, and like I have some control over my body and my life. The added benefit for me is that it helps me lose weight and keep it off.

In the Weight Watchers discussion about exercise I, too, had something to offer.

> "When I was young I thought of myself as athletic, but as the years went by I saw myself as a sedentary person. I like reading, writing, sewing, and other similar activities. My husband Bob was always busy doing something, and he would ask me to join him to help. I would think, *Okay, I'll do this physical thing, and then when I'm done I can go back to sitting and doing whatever I was doing.* Then one day I thought, *I'm going to think of this activity I'm doing with him as a fun thing we're doing together. I'm going to enjoy it for what it is.* This mindful approach, enjoying the moment I was in, was a game changer in the way I looked at physical activity. I enjoy and appreciate it more now than I ever did."

Seeing exercise as fun in and of itself was an epiphany. Saying it to others reminded me that the way I see things matters.

Regardless, sometimes I get lazy, or busy, or sick. The holidays or just the winter might derail my routine. Sometimes I just get bored with what I've been doing. Then I reboot my exercise program and revisit my priorities. I keep my workout gear, especially charged up headphones and my footwear, in a gym bag in my car. I have several pairs of athletic shoes, one for the car and one for home exercise. I also keep hiking boots in my car.

I'm always on the go and it's easy to let life get away from me. I'm a moderate exerciser and sometimes I'm better about it than other times, but exercise does make me feel better, both mentally and physically. Every time I take charge of my life, it's a mental boost.

Sleep

While having an occasional morning coffee with my sister, we talked about sleep because I'm always trying to be better about it.

> She said, "My Fitbit app says I get a good night's sleep most nights."
>
> "How?" I asked.
>
> "I go to bed in the evening between 8:00 and 8:30 and I'm asleep by 9:00 so I can get up at 5:00 a.m., do my prayers, and meditate."

I would love to do this, but honestly, this is my disciplined sister who is committed to her routines. I don't always operate that way. I set up my schedules and try to stick with it, but it's not easy and I'm only partially successful. To be fair, my sister would say it's not always easy for her either, but she is also my sister who years ago told me she loves to analyze her emotions. Maybe there's something about being open and accepting of ourselves that helps us stay healthy.

> "My app says most nights I get a fair night's sleep," I countered, "but I toss and turn and wake a lot. I keep trying to get a better night's sleep, but it's not easy."
>
> "Do you always go to bed at the same time?"
>
> "I plan to, but I might get caught up in a TV show or something I'm working on, and before I know it it's almost 10 o'clock, and I don't go to sleep till 10:30 or 11:00, which is an hour or two later than I hoped."
>
> "Do you meditate or do yoga at night?" She knew that I knew this stuff, but sometimes it's helpful to put it out there.
>
> "When I think about it. I'm working on it," was my sheepish response.

When I do have a good night's sleep, I feel great the next day, I stick more closely with healthy eating and am much more likely to exercise. My head is clear and I get more done. But, my health journey is a work in progress. I'm not perfect, but I'm always trying to improve, which is the important thing. I'll say again, it's not always easy. That's true for everything, for all of us. Sometimes it's easy, sometimes it's not. Do it anyway.

Social

Living in community with others is vitally important to our mental health.

On a YouTube video from the Desmond Tutu Peace Foundation of the deceased South African Bishop Desmond Tutu, he said (Tutu, D, 2013),[6]

> "You cannot be human on your own. You are human through relationship" (Tutu, 2012, 0:01-0:13). "Teachers of psychology tell us that we wouldn't be able to speak as human beings, we speak by imitating other human beings, we walk as human beings by imitating other human beings, we think and so ultimately, yes, we *are* human only through relationship." (Tutu, 2013, 0:30-1:01).

Ubuntu is the African word he was referring to. The communal harmony that Bishop Tutu describes is also found in the Ubuntu translation (Tutu, D. 2012),[7]

> "Ubuntu: I am because we are" (Tutu, 2012, 0:34-0:49).

Even when I want to isolate myself, I know I need others, so I have cultivated an expanded social network by volunteering in ways I care about. I have a church family whom I serve and who hold me up and pray for me when I need it. I only spend time with those who support me and make me feel good. I include my strong social contacts. I avoid places that are a draw on my energy, where I feel out of control, overwhelmed, or taken advantage of.

There are also places I feel it's important to show up and serve to be the kind of person I want to be, but I know now that I have to have healthy boundaries to not be overwhelmed. I try to spend more time with the people and in the environments that lift my spirit. I give my time and energy where I want to serve.

Identifying people and communities who make me feel particularly good or where I like to spend my time helps me see how much I have to be grateful for.

Spiritual

I've experienced loss throughout my life, from the loss of my grandmother when I was eleven, to my brother's death in the years leading up to my PTSD. More recently the deaths of my mother and my husband have left me feeling somewhat adrift. There's always a hole that's left when someone close to you dies. But even with all my experience of grief, some of my hardest times were in the months after I was raped, when my world was imploding. I was only twenty-five.

One night I felt so alone I lay on my bed in my apartment in gut wrenching anguish. More than a thousand miles separated me from all of my loved ones and I felt abandoned. I sobbed so intensely that my throat ached and finally I cried out, "God, please help me. Please don't leave me alone."

In that very instant an incredible calm descended over me. I felt God's arms wrap around me. I felt it on my skin. I was like a baby in its mother's arms, completely at peace. I knew at that moment as I was being held and rocked. I knew that *I am a child of God*. This knowledge has been a great source of love, strength, and peace in my life.

I have spent years reading about and exploring all forms of faith and prayer and its impact on our lives. I think about faith groups who promote love and caring and goodness, and faith groups who seem to be divisive and about power and control over others. I avoid faith traditions that don't promote acceptance and peace. I personally don't see how those traditions help any of us. My personal belief is that all faiths that see God as love and acceptance are all part of what God is.

My faith in God and my spirituality is a beautiful resource even in my most difficult moments. I have received affirmation when I needed it that I am not alone. Miracles happen and I am thankful that even in my darkest times, I have recognized God with me.

Mental Health

This book has detailed my journey of assault and descent into PTSD and then trying to work my way out of the resulting mental illness I suffered. My goal in therapy was to be rid of the PTSD symptoms, my anxiety and depression, and my general feeling that I was a little bit crazy. My therapist also had a goal of introducing me to my full range of emotions, something I didn't quite understand. Rion knew, however, that I needed to be comfortable feeling and expressing emotions to be able to maintain a healthy life.

Even when my mental health issues were resolved, I would still endure periods of depression. I finally realized that I had situational depression. It would emanate from something that I was embarrassed by, that I would bury away because I couldn't stand to think about it. Sometimes the thoughts persevered to the point of anxiety and shame. I often hadn't done anything that I needed to be ashamed of, I just beat myself up until I was ashamed.

My therapist, colleagues, friends, and family often commented that I was incredibly hard on myself. I was secretly proud of that fact. It meant to me that I was tough, self-sufficient, and had high expectations of myself. I am not proud of that anymore.

I still don't like to talk about the hard stuff. I might keep thinking about it, but even if I can't hide it from myself, I definitely want to hide it from everybody else. That's a lie of depression, that we can keep things to ourselves and we'll be okay. That realization has been very important for me. Now, while it's difficult, I do talk about the hard stuff, because I know it's what I have to do to achieve healing.

That's my life now on the managed side of depression, although I don't actually think I suffer from depression anymore. I'm living a self-actualized life. I'm grateful for my good fortune and most of the time I'm happy. I'm confident in myself, all of me: the good, the bad and the ugly. I now know how important it is to give ourselves grace.

My therapist, Rion, showed me the way. He helped me transform myself so I was ready for Bob. Bob helped me realize, through our many talks together, that I can talk through my being ashamed. He always showed me grace. Of all of the gifts Bob gave me, I think that is perhaps the greatest. I learned to fully accept myself. Living and maintaining a healthy life full of richness is now my goal for the rest of my life, and I know what I have to do for myself.

CHAPTER 22

Wisdom

No one gets as far as I have in life without some hard times. While recording my journey, I thought it would be interesting to ask other people with long life experiences what wisdom they had gained from their own difficult times.

After the trauma of the sudden death of an adult child, one friend told me he's learned to be more compassionate and understanding with others in general, especially those going through difficult times. He continued, "I've also learned that it is very important to treat people well and with respect. I guess I always knew that, but didn't really understand the importance of it until I had one of those bad times. I realized that I have more friends than I ever knew and they can be very helpful." He said in those difficult days and months that putting one foot in front of the other will get you through, along with faith in God and yourself. With faith and perseverance you will make it, despite it all.

While enduring the breakup of a long-time marriage, a friend told me, "I'm still not good at it some days, but I have learned the value of listening and I have learned patience."

One of my dearest friends said to me, "Even the hardest stuff in your life you learn from. Then sometimes things turn out better than you ever expected. Most importantly, I learned you can't control life."

An interesting and successful retired gentleman said he learned in his early life that you have to work hard for your goals—your dreams don't just come true; you have to decide what is worth the effort, plan your course and follow through. However, he couldn't prevent the love of his life from dying after a long and beautiful marriage. Their life was a testament to their efforts. But from that experience, he learned that even with all his hard work, you can't control everything.

Some teachers who had finished a long and purpose-filled career were on a multistate bike trip when I ran into them. After conversing for a bit I asked what wisdom they had gained from their years working with children. They both said, "Love is the answer. It's the most important thing. It has to be love."

People's perspectives either enrich or diminish their lives. My own philosophy for living a good life has been realized by my years of observing and counseling people and thinking about life in general. My perspective is informed by my nurturing family, my joy in my children and grandchildren, being in therapy, and living with Bob.

The current cultural climate in which I am writing contributes to my perspective as well. It appears to me that there are two ways of looking at life and relationships with our fellow man. First, there is a perspective of resentment; seeing the things that are hard, things we don't like about ourselves, things we don't like in others. People I care about, young people I've worked with, and even I, have fallen prey to resentment. It may not be a perspective on everything in life, but there can be a pervasive feeling that a part of our own life is completely beyond our control and that nothing is going as we want. We may resent our spouse, our kids, our parents, our siblings, our coworkers, our neighbors, our job, our money, our government, our weight, our chores and other responsibilities. The opportunity is there to be resentful about anything and everything, and some people are. I was. There is a lie that says there are big deficits in our lives and we aren't getting our due and we should focus on everything we are not, everything we don't have, everything we can't control, and everyone and everything that isn't just the way we want. We focus on the negative stuff and listen to other people who focus on everything they see as wrong. But in doing so, we don't feel better. We feel anger, negativity and resentment because life isn't our version of perfect. The truth is, the world is not perfect. None of us has all the answers, and each of us sees things from our own unique perspective.

We do have the freedom to choose our perspective, and luckily, there is a second choice. We can be resentful about the bad things, or we can be grateful for the good things.

About eight years ago, an amazing realization snuck up on me in the way I experienced gratitude. Bob and I were by the lake that is near our house. It was a warm sunny day, and I was sitting by the water feeling happy, grateful that I could be there, that the water was calm, the sun was shining, and the air was warm. I was grateful for our little shabby cottage we were living in for the summer. I was feeling grateful for Bob and all the people in my life, the ones I love, those who are my friends, people I was working with.

I returned to our cottage and said to Bob,

> "I'm so grateful lately. It's just such a lovely feeling. I'm not sure where it's coming from."
>
> Bob replied, "You have good things because you've worked hard for them. You deserve to be grateful."

"It's not that," I said. "It's not that I feel like I deserve all of this stuff. I just feel happy to be living in it. I'm happy to be sitting under a tree. I'm happy that the sun is shining, and I'm happy to see clouds. There's so much that I can enjoy. I seem to have suddenly chosen to appreciate everything instead of wanting stuff I don't have or wanting more. It's like the hard stuff doesn't matter and the simple things in life are what I'm appreciating. It's a delightful way to feel."

"You've spent your life helping others, trying to lift others up," my darling husband said. "You've told me you always knew that was your purpose. I'm glad you are turning that toward yourself now."

Since then, and especially post-therapy, I always try to choose to be grateful. Bob and I both felt that our lives had meaning. We both felt a strong sense of purpose and Bob was extremely active and involved in his work and the community. He was most proficient at pursuing his goals. He showed me in more concrete ways how to pursue doing the things in life that were important to me, to be who I felt called to be. It's not always easy. It required that I take action, that I be responsible to myself to fulfill that need.

I recently read *Man's Search for Meaning* by Viktor Frankl.[8] Frankl was a Viennese psychiatrist who was imprisoned in German concentration camps during World War II. He detailed his experience surviving four different concentration camps and the attributes that contributed to prisoners' attempts to endure the horrors they experienced. He developed Logotherapy, a theory of psychology, which I was first introduced to in college.

> "Logotherapy focuses…on the meanings to be fulfilled by the patient in his future." He wrote, "This striving to find a meaning in one's life is the primary motivational force in man" (Frankl, 2006, pp. 98-99).

Finding our meaning in life and pursuing our purpose is harder than sitting around reading a book, which I really like to do. But I think working at fulfilling my purpose is also fulfillment for me and why gratitude just turned up in my life. It's my state of being now, even when times are hard.

In the years before I met Bob, I had been hiding. I couldn't lift myself up, so I made the difficult choice to seek help. While I always had known that my purpose in life was to help others, I had not accepted help myself. I was afraid of being vulnerable and mistakenly thought that vulnerability equated to weakness. But I took responsibility for myself, reached out and found an opportunity to work with Rion in therapy. With his help, I worked hard in therapy at becoming a more self-aware, self-actualized person. With time and hard work, I stopped hiding. I started again to recognize the good in my life.

When I began to see things through the lens of gratitude I became happier, healthier, and more resilient. It has been one of the greatest gifts for me. I see the good in my life and the wonderful relationships I have. Even with the difficulty of my past, I am free from resentment. Being free from resentment has freed me from blaming others and from self-blame. I realize there is good and bad in everyone and everything but I focus on the good. I live a happy and meaningful life.

I have always known that the reason I had a relationship with Bob, that I got to be a part of his spectacular life, is that I accepted the responsibility and opportunity to take care of myself. Understanding that hard stuff always comes has helped me get through those difficult times and still be grateful for what I have. I have never stopped being grateful for that man in my life because even though he's gone now, he left me better than he found me. And he used to say the same of me. He lived his life in gratitude as well.

I am going to close with an acknowledgement to the other man, who gave me back the life I was meant to live before I closed it up in a closet for those many years. Rion saved me. I've always viewed him as my rescuer, since my darkest days. In the midst of many excruciatingly long sessions, he patiently sat in silence with me, passively encouraging me to be brave and talk. He responded whenever I called him in distress and managed to fit me into his already packed schedule on more than a few occasions. He never directed the dialogue unless I uttered the magic words, "I need help," and then suddenly he'd be animated, sit up straighter, and he would help me talk. He could see what I needed: to feel safe enough to talk, to find my emotions again, to feel, to be brave, to reach out to others for support, to put myself first sometimes, to realize life isn't for us to control—life is to live. I could not have done it on my own, I wasn't that brave. I learned all of that and more with Rion. I hope everyone who needs therapy finds a therapist as excellent as mine was.

And ultimately, it was my choice to stick with it. My life began again by braving therapy.

ACKNOWLEDGMENTS

Rion Kweller, thank you for stepping beyond your therapist role to encourage me in my writing, even while still looking out for my mental health. Your copies of the letters I sent to you and some of your therapy notes enlightened me even twenty years after the fact. Thank you for sending them to me and allowing me to use some of them in the book. During therapy, I often wondered what you were writing and I think a glimpse into the perspective of the therapist is helpful. I also sincerely appreciate your time reading this manuscript to be sure I didn't misrepresent you. Thank you for the kind words you sent me afterward.

Chandler Bolt, founder and CEO of SelfPublishing. com, whose Facebook writing hackathon walked me through everything I needed to know and do to hammer out my rough draft. An added note: the SelfPublishingSchool.com working conference in Austin, TX in June, 2022, was awesome and introduced me to my first posse of writer friends along with music playlists that I still write to.

Lisa Kroemer, my insightful and straight-talking friend. Your first read and honest critique of my rough draft intended to help people stick with therapy required that I reconsider writing my own story. It slowed up my progress, but I think now this is a book worth reading. I like your title suggestion, "Shit Happens."

John Feig, you are an inspiration to me and a wealth of knowledge. You're like having my own chatbot, referring me to podcasts and blogs about writing as well as giving me feedback on how I could present my ideas in a more compelling way. Our discussions about our family dynamics and how to approach that difficult material have been incredibly helpful. I know you take in a vast number of audio books and blogs at three times the speed of most of us, but I hope you'll slow it down a bit for this one—it's taken me years to write it.

Karen Pina, my wonderful selfpublishing.com writing/publishing coach. Thanks for your patience and care leading me on this writing journey...and for holding my feet to the fire.

Terrence Feig, my dear first husband and father of my boys. Thank you for reading the finished manuscript and the story as I told it. You were always open about your own shortcomings while I struggled with being that honest. Your loving and generous support of me in the telling of this story and some of the uncomfortable parts of our marriage is appreciated beyond words.

Alix Gilman and Elizabeth Feig, thank you for early reads of my work and encouragement that I had a compelling story and should keep writing.

Romina Cavagnola of Alchemy of Alignment Publishing, thank you for all the constructive feedback you gave me on my writing and how I could bring it alive. I really appreciate your attention to the craft.

Christina Bagni, Editor in Chief at Wandering Words Media. I learned so much in this editing process and your kind words about my writing lifted my spirits about the story I've told and the value of this book. Thank you for making the manuscript so much better.

Dr. P, who unwittingly initiated my writing this story through our discussions about the repercussions of rape.

I also want to acknowledge all of my (many) siblings for their support in my most difficult years, especially—

John Zimmerman, my older brother, for showing up when I needed you—always.

Mary Z. Robinson, for all our conversations that greatly informed my perspectives on my life around therapy and to this day, your wonderful caregiving, when I needed that.

Joanne Zimmerman, for always coming, whenever I've needed you. You just listened or stayed by my side when that's what I needed. Also—you are full of fun, which we all need sometimes.

CJ Zimmerman, my youngest brother, a sheriff's investigator who let me know this book and my experience is important. CJ told me that knowing what happened and how it affected me has informed his approach throughout his career when interviewing and working with rape survivors. Finding out that my story might have helped others before I ever wrote a word has been a big encouragement.

ENDNOTES

1. Brown, B. (2019, April 19). *Brené Brown: The Call to Courage* [Video]. Netflix. (13:43-15:27, 15:47-16:05, 17:14, 17:59, 33:53) https://www.netflix.com/us/title/81010166?s=i&trkid=258593161&vlang=en&clip=81216361.

2. Roosevelt, T. (1910, April 23). *Citizen in a Republic: The Man in the Arena* [Speech at the Sorbonne, Paris, France]. Theodore Roosevelt Center at Dickinson State University. https://www.theodorerooseveltcenter.org/Learn-About-TR/TR-Encyclopedia/Culture-and-Society/Man-in-the-Arena.aspx.

3. (1971). *Webster's Third New International Dictionary* (1971st ed., p. 2456). Merriam Webster.

4. (1971). *Webster's Third New International Dictionary* (1971st ed., p. 2456, 5b Boy Scout Handbook). Merriam Webster.

5. (1971). *Webster's Third New International Dictionary* (1971st ed., p. 816, 2a(1)). Merriam Webster.

6. Tutu, D (Desmond Tutu Peace Foundation) 2013, April 30, *We are Human Only Through Relationships:UBUNTU* (video) YouTube https://www.youtube.com/watch?v=bx_rSHNEt-g.

7. Tutu, D (Desmond Tutu Peace Foundation) 2012, December 15, *Ubuntu: A Brief Description* (Video) YouTube https://www.youtube.com/watch?v=wg49mvZ2VSU&t=29s.

8. *Frankl, V. E. (2006). Man's Search for Meaning (2006th ed., pp. 98-99). Beacon Press.*